T0193315

Echoes

ECHOES

The Boudhanath Teachings

THINLEY NORBU

Translated by William Koblensky

SHAMBHALA *Boulder · 2016*

Shambhala Publications, Inc.
4720 Walnut Street
Boulder, Colorado 80301
www.shambhala.com

Printed in the United States of America

∞ This edition is printed on acid-free paper that meets the
American National Standards Institute z39.48 Standard.

♲ Shambhala Publications makes every effort to print on recycled paper.
For more information please visit www.shambhala.com.

Shambhala Publications is distributed worldwide by Penguin Random
House, Inc., and its subsidiaries.

Designed by Michael Russem

LIBRARY OF CONGRESS CATALOGING-IN-PUBLICATION DATA
Names: Thinley Norbu, author. | Shakya Dorje, translator.
Title: Echoes: the Boudhanath teachings / Thinley Norbu; translated
    by William Koblensky.
Description: First Shambhala edition. | Boulder: Shambhala, 2016. |
Previously published: Kathmandu: Lhundrub Teng, 1977. | Translated
    from Tibetan.
Identifiers: LCCN 2015013728 | ISBN 9781611803020 (paperback:
    alk. paper)
Subjects: LCSH: Thinley Norbu—Sermons. | Buddhist sermons. |
    BISAC: RELIGION / Buddhism / Tibetan. | RELIGION / Buddhism /
    General (see also PHILOSOPHY / Buddhist).
Classification: LCC BQ7612 .T48 2016 | DDC 294.3/420423—dc23 LC
    record available at http://lccn.loc.gov/2015013728

CONTENTS

Note to the Reader   *vii*

1. Same Taste   1

2. Modes of Consciousness   17

3. Nine Vehicles   31

4. Karma   45

5. Buddhahood   61

6. Trusting the Lama   77

7. Refuge   97

8. Actual Recognition   105

9. Aspects of Buddhahood   115

10. Tantra in Action   129

11. Ethics without Concepts   145

12. Games   153

NOTE TO THE READER

The first edition of *Echoes* (Kathmandu: Lhundrub Teng, 1977) was published privately in a printing of one hundred copies with ivory-colored cloth covers. The book is based on a teaching given in Tibetan by Kyabje Thinley Norbu Rinpoche to a small group of Westerners in 1977 in Boudhanath, Nepal, with some Bhutanese and Tibetans present. This teaching had been requested by Colonel Penjo Ongdi and Aum Choden of Bhutan, who were students of Rinpoche's father, Kyabje Dudjom Rinpoche. The interpreter was William Koblensky (also known as Shakya Dorje), whose translation was transcribed from recordings of the teaching, and these transcripts were later edited to create the book. The present edition has received additional, conservative editing to update vocabulary and harmonize some details of the translation with Rinpoche's style in English.

Echoes

1 · Same Taste

I am very happy to be here today. I've recently returned from the West, where I met a lot of different people and in general received a very positive impression. There was no special reason for me to feel that way, but perhaps as a result of habits from previous lives, I liked the West and Westerners.

I have spent the greater part of my life in the East and so have always been involved in Eastern social customs, which are very rigid and restrictive. I have also been involved in the tradition of Dharma, which is also in its own way quite rigorous. Some of the people I met in the West were involved in Dharma and some were not. I found that a lot of the people not involved in Dharma are simple people with very good minds. I also found that some Westerners practicing Dharma are actually being harmed by it—their minds are deteriorating. A lot of people I met who are not involved in Dharma are very direct and straightforward, without many thoughts, doubts, or worries. Many people involved in Dharma, on the other hand, have a lot of doubts and worries and are not exactly straightforward. This made me think that perhaps in some ways it's better not to practice Dharma. Buddha Shakyamuni said that the source of all Dharma is directness, and in my experience people who know nothing of Dharma often tend to be very direct. Having learned a great deal about Dharma, people tend to become involved in the artificiality of mental fiction and so become much less direct. The teachings of Dharma have in fact taken them away from Dharma.

In the tantras and in Dzogchen it is said that one must leave awareness alone, naked, without doing anything to it, and without creating anything artificial whatsoever. A great many people who have heard a lot about Dharma can never do this; they are always creating a lot of artificial conceptions. But people who have heard nothing of Dharma do not tend to create artificial conceptions, and I think it would be easy for them to leave their awareness alone and as it is, because they have not created anything to obscure it.

I do not consider myself a Lama and so I am not [currently] wearing robes. I do not feel that I should adopt the role of a master. My father, Dudjom Rinpoche,* is a very great yogi with supremely accomplished qualities and has no pride about them whatsoever, but merely being the son of a great yogi doesn't make one special. Buddha Shakyamuni himself was the greatest of teachers, and Devadatta was certainly his cousin, yet it did not benefit Devadatta to be the cousin of Buddha Shakyamuni; he was simply a demon. Merely having a great father doesn't make me anything special. I'm approaching these talks as your friend. I enjoy talking with friends about Dharma, and this way may even be useful. A friend's qualities are not particularly relevant or important. In his previous lives, Buddha Shakyamuni even took teachings from hunters.

While I was in the West I noticed that Dharma is being spread there quite a lot. Many people are practicing Zen, and many others are involved in the four sects of Tibetan Buddhism—the Sakya, Gelug, Kagyu, and Nyingma. I am worried that Westerners will experience many obstacles in their Dharma practice. Although it's good that Dharma spreads, if Westerners are not capable of practicing it very well, Dharma will primarily become an obstacle for them. So if we persevere in our practice, we will further the spread of Dharma.

Teaching Dharma is not easy. We must recognize that there are many different kinds of people, and different people have different faculties. This leads to different approaches to Dharma and to inclinations toward different types of practice. There are Hinayana types, to whom one should teach the Hinayana; Mahayana types, to whom one should teach the Mahayana; and Vajrayana types, to whom one should teach the Vajrayana. There are people who are capable of having a good relationship with primordial wisdom, to whom one should teach wisdom; there

---

*Kyabje Dudjom Jikdral Yeshe Dorje Rinpoche (skyabs rje bdud 'joms 'jigs bral ye shes rdo rje rin po che, 1904–1987).

are people who have philosophical inclinations, to whom one should teach philosophy; and so on. I am not capable of seeing what kind of people you are and what kind of faculties you have, so I would like to ask what particular interests and aspirations you have in Dharma.

How can Dharma be practiced without such exterior signs as wearing robes and doing prostrations? You seem to have implied that these things are not necessary.

I did not mean that these things have no purpose. The point is that Dharma is intended to benefit the mind, so whatever one does in Dharma is likewise intended to benefit the mind. If a particular practice is beneficial to the mind, then it is positive. Therefore, if practices such as doing prostrations and setting up an altar and making offerings and repeating the Dorje Sempa [Vajrasattva] mantra benefit the mind, one should definitely do them. They can all benefit the mind. Buddha Shakyamuni said that all phenomena are an expression of the mind. The mind is the most important thing to work with in Dharma. So one's basic frame of reference in any Dharma practice is working with and transforming the mind, and whatever furthers that intention is an appropriate activity in Dharma.

Rinpoche, what kind of people did you meet in the West other than Dharma people? When you say simple people, do you mean, for example, people who work on buses, farmers, and so on?

Yes, I met people like that. I also went out into the countryside and met country people, and I found them very direct and simple. In this way they had very good minds.

I'm not in any way formally educated, but it seems to me that education may be an obstacle to Dharma practice. Prolonged formal education may tend to reinforce your attachment to your own mind.

No, no; the obstacles are in the nature of the people who are studying Dharma. We find almost the same syndrome in both East and West. The qualities of Dharma are quite difficult to develop, but if one has a lot of merit and practices very hard, one can eventually develop outer qualities for the benefit of others, and inner qualities of understanding.

If we develop both of these, we will be able to benefit others, but this is quite difficult.

When people are involved in Dharma, they often try to learn and understand things. They come to know more than other people and are finally called scholars. Then they acquire a reputation for knowing something, so they become proud. These individuals may go on studying and may even become extremely learned. If one continues in this fashion, one will eventually acquire a lot of intellectual understanding about Dharma and will be able to explain it precisely and make accurate judgments. This approach may lead to a greater tendency to intensify one's pride. This makes it difficult to train the mind and attain understanding. Without developing inner and outer qualities through recognizing the nature of mind, and attaining understanding from that, one will not really be able to benefit other people no matter how learned one may have become. This is a problem one finds equally in the East and in the West.

Could you give some teachings on the essence of the mind—how to understand it, see it, and meditate on it?

What I'm going to say doesn't really have much to do with the practice of the Dharma, but I think it's important anyway and I'd like to talk about it. When we begin to practice Dharma, we have a choice about exactly how to approach it, and this is a very important choice. Whenever we set out to do anything, we always have a choice right at the beginning about how to approach it, and how we make that choice will determine how we work through the situation. In approaching Dharma, one might decide to study and gain a strong intellectual comprehension of it. An approach like this would concentrate entirely on study. If one sets out to do this, one can actually achieve one's aim and finally understand a great deal about Dharma. However, in the final outcome, this will not really be of any great benefit.

The other choice is to try and integrate a certain amount of learning with the practice of Dharma. In this approach one would receive a few instructions on Dharma and practice them. This is called *mintri* in Tibetan.* *Min* means "to bring to fruition" in the same way that a plant

* smin khrid.

or fruit is brought to fruition, and *tri* means "teaching"; therefore, the word *mintri* means "the teachings that bring one to fruition." Here one attempts to receive those teachings that are relevant to one's practice, and one is determined to practice those teachings constantly in order to attain realization.

All the vehicles [yanas] are very important: the Hinayana definitely constitutes the teachings of the Buddha, the Mahayana is the source of full realization, and the Vajrayana is a special branch of the Mahayana concerning method.

Some people may have aspirations to monkhood, while others prefer to practice unordained. But however we aspire to practice, it's very important not to get rigid about it. We should not be too worried about what we are doing and should not have a judgmental attitude in practicing Dharma, but should be quite relaxed and open in our approach. There is a vast expanse within Dharma. There are many, many different kinds of teaching, and there are many, many different kinds of people for whom those teachings are intended. If we are heavily judgmental and rigid about vehicles, we will tend to cut ourselves off from a lot of Dharma. Whether we are meditating, listening to teachings, or thinking about Dharma, we should always try to maintain an open and nonjudging attitude.

In Dharma practice it is important to know about the five extreme attitudes. These are not philosophical views but attitudes that confuse people, and which should be avoided. The first of these is wrong beliefs, such as holding that Dharma is not beneficial or that there is no such thing as karma or rebirth. The second is the attitude of grasping at fictitious absolutes—ideas such as "This is really it, this is the ultimate experience, this is the ultimate truth. I have understood." This should be avoided. The third is fascination with the five skandhas: one's physical form, feeling, perception, intention, and consciousness. The five skandhas have no objectifiable reality at all, so both magnifying their importance and attributing any kind of real nature to them should be avoided. The fourth is regarding our own ethics as something to be proud of. We might feel that it is very good to keep precepts and that we are improved or benefited merely by keeping them. This might lead us to become proud of our own ethics, and it would prevent them from being useful. The fifth is related to the fourth: we should not consider the mad actions of a yogi to be exemplary in themselves. There is certainly something unique in the behavior of a realized being, but this behavior has no more inherent value than keeping precepts. If people think they are virtuous just because they observe precepts, they are making a mistake. On the other hand, if they think that being a yogi exempts them from ethical behavior, that is a mistake, too. These are both self-defeating and should be avoided.

Mind itself has no objectifiable reality, but for countless lifetimes we have not recognized this. As a result, we have given rise to the notion of self, or "I." This notion of "I" is the ego. It creates its own projections, an entire sphere of its own. This sphere is nothing but the projection of the ignorant ego, but we don't recognize this and think it is something else. From this arises the duality of subject and object: the object is the world or environment we find ourselves in, and the subject is the individual or ego that regards itself as perceiving the field. This perception of "otherness" gives us the feeling of being in a multifarious environment that is external to ourselves. The relationship between the ego and its realm causes us to discriminate between what benefits and what harms. As a further result of these discriminations, we develop notions of aversion and desire. We desire things that we think are good for us, and feel aversion toward things we consider harmful. So, by not recognizing the essentially non-objectifiable nature of the mind, we have created defilements and our own confusion.

It's not particularly important whether we assume the role of a monk. What is crucial is to trust that actions have inevitable results in accordance with the working of karma. The source of all conditioned events is attachment to duality, the basic duality of an ego and the field in which the ego is structured. As long as there is duality, there are causes and results, samsara and nirvana, demons and gods, bad and good, birth and death and rebirth. Without attachment to duality, there is no cause and result, no bad and good, no samsara and nirvana—also no Dharma, no teachings, no path, and nothing whatsoever to do. Basically what we must do in Dharma practice is transcend duality. When we recognize the ego to be a fallacy, the duality of realm and ego disappears and everything becomes a field of total evenness.

We will inevitably feel that we have been improved by practicing Dharma, and that we have learned something or developed some kind of positive qualities or understanding. This may lead to feelings of pride. At the moment of feeling pride, the field of observation is that pride itself. We are caught in the dual structure of pride and ego. At that moment we should examine the nature of that pride; it could not be anything in itself. No matter how long one examines pride, one will never find anything that is pride, nor will one find any source for its arising. Furthermore, one will see that pride is not permanent, and will be less inclined to trust it. Eventually one will recognize the emptiness of the prideful conception and understand the meaning of emptiness through pride itself. On the other hand, if one allows pride to take control, one will lose the sense that there is anything wrong with dual structures. Having been caught in duality, one will assume the existence of an individual as an entity. Due to pride, an idea will arise such as "I am very learned and he doesn't know anything," and one will be insulting or aggressive. One will thus create a lot of bad karma and make others unhappy, creating difficulties for oneself and ultimately isolating oneself from the world. In this way, one will become more entangled in the web of samsara.

When feeling aversion, we should look to see where it is and why we project an object of aversion. An object of aversion is no more than a formulation of the mind. We become angry with our own projection, a projection of the ego ignorantly created through a failure to recognize the nature of mind. Therefore, we should look at the nature of the mind creating these projections. Strong tendencies to objectify and solidify a particular reality will then drift away. We will feel very relaxed, light, and happy, and we will become calm about everything.

Sometimes we feel pain and are unhappy, sometimes we meet friends and are happy, sometimes we are separated from our friends and are unhappy. Sometimes we become involved in a close relationship with someone and feel happy in that relationship, and when it breaks up we feel unhappy again. We feel sad and depressed, we can't eat, we can't sleep, and we cry, so we try to do something about it; we go out and get drunk and perhaps this makes us feel a little better. Then we come around in the morning and feel depressed again. In this way, we get involved in a cycle of suffering and happiness. When involved in such feelings, we should constantly observe the nature and condition of the mind. So when we are happy, when a relationship breaks up, or when we are separated from our friends, we should observe the nature and condition of the mind. Although we will still feel those emotions, we will also feel an evenness running through unhappiness and happiness. When happy, we will recognize emptiness through happiness, and when unhappy, we will recognize emptiness through unhappiness. This practice is called the same taste of happiness and unhappiness.

We all travel from one place to another and find ourselves in varying circumstances, some unpleasant and some pleasant. The Buddhist view is that these conditions are due not to external forces, but to our own karma. So whether involved in bad or good circumstances, we should watch the nature of the mind. We will experience the evenness running through bad and good conditions, and we will be able to recognize emptiness through them. This practice is called the same taste of bad and good conditions.

A good number of people who practice Dharma are able to overcome bad conditions, to avoid being controlled by them and work through them. But it's much more difficult to use good conditions and much easier to be controlled by good conditions than by bad ones. There are relatively few people who can work with good conditions and continue in their pure practice of Dharma.

When people become rich, when they are in comfortable circumstances and everybody considers them to be good and praises them, at those times it is difficult to feel that everything is a manifestation of the mind and mere appearance. Appearances are neither beneficial nor harmful. No appearance, however bad it may be, ever harms anything; no appearance, however good, ever improves anything.

I can't speak about the West, but certainly Easterners find it particularly difficult to deal with favorable conditions. Even if they can use bad conditions and persevere without being controlled by them, when people find themselves in favorable circumstances they really like them, are controlled by them, and lose their practice of same taste. It's especially important to handle good circumstances carefully. Someone who is practicing Dharma but hasn't developed very much in meditation might not treat a poor person particularly well. But if he met a rich person who might be useful to him, he would probably treat him considerably better. This would be a sign that he couldn't practice same taste in favorable circumstances.

All types of attitudes toward Dharma can be found wherever Dharma has been spread, but in the West I came across one that I had not observed in the East. People would say, "His Dharma practice is very good, he's very strong," and they would put a lot of emphasis on strength. From a worldly point of view, strength is certainly something that helps us get our work done, but the strength these people point out seems to be ego strength, and a tough, resilient ego isn't particularly useful in Dharma. If we continually practice same taste and so experience the evenness of all conditions, we will not be proud when we develop great qualities. We will not feel depressed or aggressive under unfavorable conditions. We will never develop pride or have an erratic nature, but will become strong through the practice of same taste. This is what is meant in Dharma by strength. Ego strength is counterproductive because ego is impermanent. However much ego strength we build up, it is impermanent and will eventually break down. By practicing same taste, we will develop the strength of egolessness. If we develop this strength, we will spontaneously recognize primordial wisdom, which will enable us to build the true strength of Dharma.

Could you say more about the difference between ego strength and diligence, Rinpoche?

As with all six paramitas, or liberating qualities, vigorous application should always be infused into any Dharma practice. In listening to Dharma here, for example, we are already practicing all six paramitas. At this time of day we would normally be relaxing and enjoying ourselves, but we gave up our time to come here and talk about Dharma—we gave some of our time, and this is *giving.* Since a mind without pride and jealousy is a pure mind and the very essence of all ethics, if we listen to the teachings without pride or jealousy, we are practicing *ethics.* While listening to the teachings we get thirsty, we feel hungry, and our knees become sore, but we willingly put up with all these difficulties. In this way we practice *patience.* Patience is not simply passive; it demands energy. Listening to the teachings in the constant awareness that we are listening to them is the practice of energy, or *diligence,* and concentrating on the importance of the teachings is the practice of *concentration.* Listening attentively to the teachings, thinking about them, and asking questions is the practice of *penetrating intuition* in listening to the teachings.*

One can integrate the six paramitas with any Dharma practice. The essence of giving is not clinging to anything. Normally we think of giving in terms of an external individual and an external object given, and this is certainly a kind of giving. But in true meditation we are not attached to anything, not even to an ego, so there can be no attachment to any ego projection. As Milarepa emphasized, this is the ultimate form of giving, for one has abandoned attachment to everything, even to the ego. In meditation one also practices ethics. When meditating, one observes the nature of mind itself, ultimately pure and beyond all conceptions of unclean and clean, bad and good. As purity is the essence of ethics, one practices ethics when meditating. From the very beginning, the fundamental nature† has no discrimination of bad or good, unhappy or happy, unpleasant or pleasant, which is the essence of patience. Vigorous application, or diligence, is generally considered to mean trying to do something, and this is vigorous application at an ordinary level. But the fundamental nature has no beginning, no end, and no present, and this transcendence of any time structure is the real nature of vigorous application. By abiding in the fundamental nature, one also practices concentration. In general we think of concentration as the mind being fixed on some object, but in this practice the fundamental nature abides by itself, as it is, and the mind reaches ultimate stability in that state. In this condition the mind can abide by itself, because the fundamental nature never changes and never wavers. It is never anything other than what it is. This is the essential quality of concentration. Emptiness is not empty like space but is an ultimate total potential that can give rise to anything. It can give rise to all possible forms, colors, and expressions. This total potential is without any clinging or attachment and does not identify anything as having any particular characteristic. This is the perfection of penetrating intuition in meditation.

*The six paramitas are translated in other writings by Kyabje Thinley Norbu Rinpoche as generosity, morality, patience, diligence, samadhi, and wisdom.

†The translator has used "fundamental nature" for *nelug* (gnas lugs), which Kyabje Thinley Norbu Rinpoche has translated variously in other writings as way of abiding, pure nature, ultimate nature, true nature, and absolute nature.

The six paramitas are a basic Mahayana teaching and apply to any kind of Dharma practice. We shouldn't be too literal about the six paramitas and think that giving only means giving objects away or that ethics only means taking particular precepts and keeping them by wearing certain robes and acting in a certain way. It is of the utmost importance to be completely open and relaxed to achieve the complete integration of the six paramitas with any Dharma practice. We will then be able to practice and understand anything whatsoever in Dharma. If we are completely open and spacious, that space will encompass the whole of Dharma. If we are rigid and closed, all the teaching we accumulate will only become a source of personal paranoia.

There are a lot of different Dharma teachings in the Tibetan tradition. Each of the four sects has many different teachings and many different Lamas, some of whom have fine qualities and understanding, and others of whom are just rigid. In approaching Dharma, it is important first to be open and second to follow an appropriate teacher. A teacher should himself be very open and should preferably have developed both the outer and inner qualities: the fundamental understanding and the qualities of expression in teaching the Dharma. If one cannot find a teacher who has developed both these qualities, a teacher who has at least developed the inner qualities of understanding can also lead one to realization. If one finds such a teacher and is open and receptive to Dharma, one will be able to embrace all the teachings, to understand Dharma, and to attain realization. But if one follows a Lama who is just rigid, all he will be able to teach is his own phenomena.

Some people have aspirations to become monks and some have aspirations to practice unordained. There is nothing wrong with either of these aspirations as long as one maintains an open mind and does not defame anyone because his approach differs from one's own. If a monk can understand Dharma and maintain an open mind, that mind will be pure and he will be able to attain realization. If an unordained practitioner maintains a sense of openness, his mind will also be pure and he too will be able to attain realization. So one should not disparage the ways of others just because they differ from one's own.

I have met a few Western monks, and from personal contact with them I'm inclined to think that Westerners possibly make better monks than

Easterners because they have the advantage of not knowing very much about Dharma. They have taken ordination, but they don't have a particularly detailed idea of their precepts, and they're not proud, because they don't know much about Dharma. Their minds are still quite open and therefore pure, so they're excellent monks. I'm not just making this up—both Buddha Shakyamuni and Milarepa said in similar terms that the absence of defilement makes a true monk. For this reason, some Westerners have become exemplary monks even though they have worn robes only recently. They don't think, "I am a very good person because I am a monk," and so they don't become proud or imagine that they have improved. They don't develop many of the defilements that would arise just through their being monks.

Among Tibetans one can find some very exemplary people, and there is certainly a lot to be learned from them. Though I would never disparage my own people, one can also learn some terrible things from Tibetans. To take one example—applicable to certain ordinary individuals but not of course to any noted Lamas—among the Gelugpas there are a number of people who dislike the Nyingma because of its large unordained following and its married Lamas. "Those people don't know how to keep their precepts," they say. "They don't know anything about Dharma because they don't have its basic source—they aren't monks and they drink a lot of alcohol." The same type of people in the Nyingma disparage the Gelugpas. They say, "The Gelugpas don't know anything about Dharma—they're nothing but a bunch of Hinayana followers who have no Mahayana or Vajrayana teachings whatsoever." This has nothing to do with Dharma, for there can be no question of one sect being superior to another. It merely proves that one can learn a lot of bad things from Tibetans.

Leave the mind in the natural condition, just as it is. Then being a monk and wearing monk's robes is good, being a Buddhist yogi and wearing white robes is also good, and not wearing any robes at all, the mind is still pure in the natural condition. The most important thing in Dharma is to purify one's mind as much as possible. Purification of the mind is the real meaning of Dharma and the basic importance of practice. It is possible to learn from many people who are involved in Dharma. It is also possible just to get a lot of ideas in one's head and distort the mind, and finally one will be incapable of leaving the mind in the natural condition. Having approached Dharma and learned many different ways of distorting the mind, not only will one have failed to benefit oneself but one will also have gone farther from Dharma.

Westerners have a great ability to leave the mind as it is because they have been doing so from an early age and start out with no preconceptions about Dharma. This is a great advantage and should not be lost—never learn how to distort the mind. Europe is a very pleasant, happy place. Even so, Westerners are traditionally hardworking. In attempting many things on a large scale, they create many desires, which in turn create a lot more work. If a person with this conditioning decides to investigate foreign culture and learns more concepts and more ways of looking at the world, he can get an overload of different ideas and may even go insane.

When you practice Dharma, try not to have too many hopes. If you wear robes, try not to have too many hopes about being a monk. Don't get into diversions like "I'm going to be a monk; now I'll be really pure and keep pure ethics." Also, when studying Dharma, try not to have too many hopes about learning anything. Don't feel, "I'm learning about Dharma; now I'm going to learn a lot." Be open. Take the attitude, "Now I'm learning something about Dharma and that's good." But don't worry about achieving anything. It's most important to keep the mind relaxed and to allow wisdom to arise spontaneously. Being rigid, worrying a lot, and creating hopes and fears prevent the arising of wisdom.

I hope that Westerners studying Dharma in the East will eventually be able to return to the West and start new Dharma customs. Westerners who have taken teachings primarily in the West, especially those who have associated with Lamas of great fame, may become proud of their association with such Lamas and with Dharma. They are often rough and bitter toward people who have studied Dharma in the East and to those not involved in Dharma. This was on my mind when I said perhaps it is better never to study or practice Dharma, for it can just make one a worse person. It is of benefit to practice Dharma and follow a Lama whether he is famous or not. But no matter how many great and famous Lamas one meets, if one does not practice Dharma according to the way it should be practiced, it will be of no benefit at all. There's an old Kagyu saying: "One must practice Dharma in accordance with Dharma. If one doesn't practice Dharma in accordance with Dharma, it becomes a source of rebirth in the lower realms."

We all face these difficulties no matter how long we've been trying to practice Dharma. In my own case, I have found that approaching many different teachings and studying a lot make me feel acquisitive and proud. I feel I should just meditate or repeat Guru Rinpoche's mantra.* Although it can be beneficial, study can also be dangerous.

Could you say a little more about the same taste of happiness and suffering?

If I found myself in favorable material circumstances and some of my friends said things like "Thinley Norbu is a great Lama," I would begin to feel proud. This pride would eventually lead me to believe these things about myself. Since pride is one of the sources of desire—pride leads to the desire to aggrandize oneself and accumulate possessions—I would begin to think I should behave in certain ways in order to elicit further responses like this from the environment. By trying to act in this way, I would create a certain amount of suffering for myself and cause conditions to deteriorate. Pride would have transformed good conditions into bad.

A number of methods for dealing with favorable conditions are taught in the different vehicles. In the Hinayana, a monk reflects upon seeing a beautiful woman that association with women is a source of confusion and of continuing in samsara. He is taught also to reflect on the disgusting nature of the body: although a woman may appear very beautiful, she is made up of flesh, bone, liver, blood, guts, and other disgusting things. There is nothing fundamentally beautiful about her at all. At the Mahayana level, a beautiful woman is considered a projection. There is no such thing as beauty. Beauty is a projection that subjective consciousness lays on particular appearances. Instead of dwelling on the beauty of any appearance, we should look at the nature of the perceiving mind and recognize fundamental emptiness. The Vajrayana teaches different levels of understanding in different tantras. Different methods of practice are also taught in the development and completion stages. While the development stage consists largely of visualizations, this is not the totality of the devel-

*OM AH HUNG VAJRA GURU PADMA SIDDHI HUNG.

opment stage or the only way to approach it by any means. There is also a method of approaching development-stage practice by what is called the effortless manifestation of inseparable form and emptiness. In this method one does not visualize or imagine anything in particular detail, but develops the attitude that from the very beginning everything is the nature of a Buddhafield and all sentient beings are the nature of Dakas and Dakinis. With this attitude one can maintain the meditation of the development stage in all situations. The attitudes of all three vehicles are Dharma approaches to favorable situations.

I traveled around America quite a lot, and I was often very happy and had many good friends. This became a source of suffering because my leaving saddened everybody. I made a lot of friends in Berkeley; when I left, everybody there became unhappy, and since I had enjoyed being with them, I was unhappy to go. I had a similar experience in Honolulu, which struck me as a very beautiful place. I often thought of my family, who were back at home in Bhutan at that point, and wondered whether they were happy. If one cannot meditate in these situations, one can involve oneself in a lot of suffering.

When I left the East for the first time and went to Europe, I was reminded of how much I am a Tibetan. In America I started to learn some English—I wasn't able to learn much, but I picked up enough to speak a little and make some contact with different people. I became used to the flexible ways of the West and felt very much at home there. Now that I have returned to the East, I find as much difficulty relating to the situation as I did on my first visit to the West. I have to relearn how to be a Tibetan, which I find somewhat uncomfortable.

I also met a lot of selfish, inconsiderate people in the West; probably everybody meets people like that. If one cannot meditate at such times, one can get involved in one's own suffering. When I encountered such people, I felt that the East is really not such a bad place. People are careful in the East and have consideration for others. If one cannot maintain one's meditation through these conditions, they will become a source of suffering. If one can meditate at these times, they will become a source of insight.

The practice of the same taste of unhappiness and happiness, or suffering and pleasure, is extremely important and very beneficial. It is best done without reference to anything substantial whatsoever. We could get drunk to relieve our suffering, and this might help a little, but we would then become dependent on alcohol for relief, and when it eventually left our system we would suffer again. Anything substantial we depend on to effect any psychological change is inherently untrustworthy because we will become dependent on it, and eventually we will be separated from it. A far better way to transform experience is to work with the mind. This involves no dependence on any substance, and as a result all experiences become a source of insight.

2 · Modes of Consciousness

Is consciousness the same thing as what we would call awareness?

Basically they're different. The term "consciousness" is applied to an ordinary individual in samsara. "Awareness," or *rigpa* in Tibetan, has two meanings: "awareness of insight" and "intellectual faculty." But what awareness really means is the wisdom of an enlightened being, something quite distinct from consciousness. Beings who have been wandering for a long time in samsara are aware only of consciousness and so continue to wander in samsara. Although awareness abides along with consciousness, our habitual reference to consciousness has prevented us from recognizing awareness. If we can find favorable conditions and meet the appropriate teacher, he will be able to indicate the nature of awareness as undifferentiated from consciousness.

I'd like to ask if it's possible to prove intellectually that shunyata, or fundamental emptiness, is knowable, or does one have to experience it?

It can certainly be intellectually proven, but proving something intellectually is still speculation. If one recognizes something directly, one sees that it's there through actual experience of it; then one knows what it is. However, people who practice Dharma must remember that it's not enough merely to recognize fundamental awareness.* One must sustain that awareness, gain confidence in it, and use it in such a way that it is never disturbed but functions in both unfavorable and favorable conditions.

*"Fundamental awareness" here is a translation of *rigpa* (rig pa), which Kyabje Thinley Norbu Rinpoche translates in other writings as "awareness" or "awareness mind."

I have often noticed that in altered states of consciousness, people testify to having different experiences of the world. I wonder if you could relate this to the Buddhist view of the five senses and consciousness. Are different modes of consciousness in any sense real or absolute?

First one should distinguish two modes of experience, individual and general.* The general experiential field appears much the same to everyone, and the individual fields appear differently to different individuals. There is no absolute way to make an exact distinction between general and individual experience, for these are variable with circumstance and individuals. Years ago there weren't many machines. Eventually someone had the idea of making a particular machine, and this became a factor in his individual experience. When the machine came to be manufactured and widely available, everyone became quite used to it, and now everyone has some conception of a watch or a car, for example. In other words, those conceptions entered the field of general experience. Although there are many factors in the mind that are general and many that are particular to each individual, it is impossible to say whether any particular one is either individual or general. Everybody in this room can see the image of the Buddha—this is an example of general experience. If I thought about an image of Padmasambhava, that would form a part of my individual experience rather than my general experience, since there is no particular reason for anyone else to be thinking about Padmasambhava.

Which do you think is less erroneous, general or individual?

Both come into activity constantly; you move from one to the other. It seems that most people work on an individual basis and perceive at their own level, but they also check on the general perception to see their own relationship to it.

No, general consciousness is a fallacy. Each individual experiences without reference to anyone else. He does not share anyone else's experience.

If somebody here died, everyone else would still perceive the details of the room. This seems to demonstrate that there is some sort of general

---

*Translated in other writings by Kyabje Thinley Norbu Rinpoche as "general and personal phenomena."

consciousness. If most people considered their own perceptions to be the most important, how would we function in an organized way? An election, for example, requires general agreement on how it is to be run.

Each person has to deal with his individual perception first and then check it against the general perception. That is the way most people decide whether or not they are crazy.

Don't you think social experience is very strong? If there were a bottle and some glasses here and I poured a drink for everyone, we would all agree that we were drinking water. One person would not be drinking water and somebody else drinking fire. We can consider also something like social organization: how could we have social organization without social experience? How would there be any connection between sentient beings if there were no social experience?

These are just nominalizations; they have no inherent reality. Of course, from a Madhyamaka point of view there is no existence anyway, but from a practical point of view these are just nominalizations. We say we have a shared experience, but blue to me is a different thing from blue to you.

This is in accordance with the idea that beings in different realms have different perceptions. For example, a fish perceives water as a dwelling, a human being perceives it as something to drink, and a god perceives it as a completely different substance, as amrita.

In fact, this sort of discussion is just a game. The distinction between social and individual is merely functional, and no meaningful distinction between the two can be made at all. For practical purposes it is sometimes necessary to make the distinction, but the truth that is free from error is neither of these—it is inherent wisdom or awareness. In recognizing this awareness and continually connecting to it, we discover what is erroneous. The very distinction between outer and inner disappears, and with it the division between inner experience and outer experience, and no basis for anything like a duality of social and individual remains. Therefore, the so-called social and individual experiences are equally untrustworthy, as both are based on ignorance. Only awareness has any reality.

There are a lot of different doctrines and traditions of philosophy and belief in the world. Which type is more correct, that which many people accept or that which only a few accept?

That's like a lot of boats that are all going to sink in a whirlpool in the middle of a river. There are big boats for people who want to drown in company and small boats for people who prefer to drown alone, but everyone's going to drown.

Whatever doctrine is congruent with the absolute truth is the truth, regardless of whether a lot of people believe it or not.

What kind of standard can be used to establish the validity of a particular philosophy?

Individual recognition and realization of the truth.

The individual mind is fundamentally false.

The experience of the nature of reality.

That is impossible. No one could ever realize the truth. The very individual who set out to do so would himself be an error—how could he ever realize anything? At one time it was said that the entire population of India was in agreement on all the policies of Indira Gandhi. Only a short time later, the entire population of India appeared to be in agreement on the faults of the policies of Indira Gandhi. This shows the quality of consensus opinion.

They could have changed. Logic would tell them if something was incorrect.

Certainly they would have changed. But anything subject to change could not be real; it must be erroneous.

Surely if one looks at this question of the validity of a system from a Tibetan Buddhist point of view, the important factor is the capability of the individual. Generally it is said that the Buddha taught the different yanas according to the capabilities of different individuals: the Hinayana for those of lower abilities, the Mahayana for those of medium abilities, and the Vajrayana for those of the highest abilities. On this basis one can say that since more people follow the Hinayana, probably the popularity of a system goes along with lower capabilities. In other words, whatever is most popular is least true.

This is more or less the point: it is irrelevant how many people agree on a particular viewpoint. Agreement creates a social force—people think their tradition and their viewpoint are very pure, very correct, and become defensive about them. This does not prove anything. Any viewpoint formulated intellectually, created by an ordinary consciousness, is bound to be erroneous. That ordinary consciousness itself is fundamentally erroneous, so any viewpoint of philosophy based on it must equally be mistaken. Only a statement based on wisdom could be true or real in any meaningful sense.

Nevertheless, the force of social consciousness seems to be rather strong today. There is a general feeling among a large number of people that ideas which have become generally accepted must be more true than ideas held by only a few people. Perhaps the Nyingmapas and Bönpos could be considered numerically rather small, and one might criticize them on these grounds. One might say that something must be wrong with their outlook since few people seem to agree with them. This has nothing to do with the truth or validity of their viewpoint. In fact, I know very little about the Bönpos today, so I cannot make any judgments about them, but certainly the size of their population does not mean that their views have no validity. The presence of wisdom imparts meaning to a system, and one based only on speculative thought is inherently erroneous.

People who have a lot of authority and are used to large undertakings set out in their work with the confidence that they know what they are doing. People who are not used to these things, on the other hand, feel a lot of hesitation and even fear upon approaching the same situations. This is analogous to a relationship with wisdom. The capable and confident individual carries out his work despite the fact that most people would not be able to do it. This corresponds with the truth of the view of wisdom and the error of the view of consciousness. The notion that a belief is validated merely by being accepted in society is an attitude based on delusion and has no meaning in Dharma.

The only reference that has meaning in Dharma is the reference to wisdom. However, if we have only a reference to fundamental awareness but have not developed confidence in it, we may find ourselves in conflict with others. Even though we may have faith in Dharma and some insight, when we come into contact with people who do not share our experience and opinions, we may be negatively influenced and even lose our awareness—we may fall under the control of what seems to be the general experience. We must develop confidence in fundamental awareness as well as recognize it.

Chandrakirti illustrated the foolishness of deciding any question on the basis of consensus with the following story, held to be historical. It is said that a certain Indian king was advised by his astrologer that an intoxicating rain would fall in a week's time. The king became concerned about this and ordered a big roof built over his well without announcing anything to his subjects. When the rains came, everyone who drank the water became intoxicated, and the intoxication they experienced gave them all similar conceptions, but because the king's frame of consciousness had not been altered by drinking the rainwater, the people thought he had become insane. This general agreement about the king's insanity made him quite depressed, so eventually he too drank some rainwater and became intoxicated. Then all the people said, "Ah! Now we see that the king has not really become insane at all."

In the Nyingma tradition, saving all sentient beings from suffering is described in terms of one's own perception. This means that the field that we experience as "other" is based on the perception of a "self," and social experience is based on individual experience. This does not make individual experience or the individual himself any more important, however, and individual perception remains erroneous. But if one can recognize fundamental awareness, the basis of one's own perception, one can transform individual experience into wisdom and therefore attain realization. With the attainment of this freedom of wisdom, there is no longer any erroneous projection of an external world. Ceasing to project an erroneous external world is called "saving all sentient beings from suffering in terms of one's own perception."

The world is full of ignorant sentient beings who commit all sorts of crimes. How should society deal with that sort of thing?

In the perception of a Buddha, there are no criminals. There is also no society, no police, no controls at all. We are not Buddhas and so do not perceive in this way, but as people seeking realization we must look for the path. We must appreciate how to move toward realization and understand our position in terms of realization. People who are not involved in trying to attain realization have to obey the norms of society and function in accordance with its general rules. Those who are practicing the path must also function in terms of the norms of society but should not allow their outlook to be governed by those norms. Laws are based only on a very rough appreciation of social structure. The black market gets a lot of criticism in the East, and sometimes there is a big cleanup and many black marketers are imprisoned. This, we are told, is very good for the country, but it also harms those who are benefited by the black market.

There is a story about the Buddha in a previous life killing a person who was planning to murder five hundred merchants. The Buddha wanted to prevent the murder of these five hundred people and also to save the potential murderer from his own karma.

That story illustrates the difference between Hinayana and Mahayana ethics. The last three of the ten unvirtuous actions are entirely mental, so committing them is necessarily unvirtuous. But since the other seven concern body and speech, the Hinayana approach to ethical precepts is only a general indication, not an absolutely fixed rule, and sometimes it is even necessary to violate the ethical precepts if the circumstances warrant it. Mahakarunika, one of the previous incarnations of Buddha Shakyamuni, was traveling with five hundred merchants who were all incarnations of Bodhisattvas. Mahakarunika recognized that the bandit would create a great deal of unvirtuous karma and fall into the hells by killing these Bodhisattvas. Killing the bandit prevented him from creating bad karma and was essentially a virtuous action because it was performed without selfish motivation or desire. This is a Mahayana approach to ethics. In the Mahayana it is sometimes appropriate to perform actions of body and speech normally considered unvirtuous, provided that the situation calls for it and one's motivation is pure. However, since mental events are confined entirely within the mind, there is no reason ever to commit a mentally unvirtuous action. There is no time when a mentally unvirtuous action can be anything other than unvirtuous.

Would it have made any difference if the five hundred merchants hadn't been incarnations of Bodhisattvas?

It would still have been a virtuous action to kill him even if the merchants had not been incarnations of Bodhisattvas. Mahakarunika saved the lives of five hundred people, although he had to take the life of one individual to do it. This was not just an arbitrary choice. He acted out of his Bodhisattva vow to aid all beings, taking no regard for his own condition.

How should society react to a Hitler?

From a Jewish point of view, Hitler was certainly a demonic individual who murdered a great many Jews. From the point of view of a Nazi, Hitler benefited the whole world. Such an issue is problematical because there are two large groups with completely opposite views; indeed, social questions inevitably lead to political division. Therefore, we come back to the initial point, that social conceptions are always erroneous, and no more than creations of the mind.

Society is simply an aggregate of individual choices. For instance, our friend here likes to be a monk, drinks tea, and never touches alcohol. He prefers to live that way. I like to have women around, and have a drink in the evening. Like children, we both do what we want.

So it's okay if I put DDT around my place to get rid of the fleas?

If you have no dualistic conceptions whatsoever, you can kill them, but if you do have dualistic conceptions, you shouldn't.

Infants like to play in ashes and mud and so on, and they don't see anything wrong in this. From their point of view it seems like the perfect thing to do. But from an older person's point of view this seems wrong or immature. As people grow up they like to drink and have parties, laugh, talk, and have a lot of fun. This seems to be just the thing to do, and appears to have some meaning. But from the point of view of older people these ways are frivolous and mistaken. What they consider important is to run a business, read the newspaper, and be serious about things, and they consider throwing parties and having fun to be wrong.

Then there are Buddhists. Buddhists often consider that those involved in business or a work routine are falling into traps because they are growing old and haven't practiced Dharma: they don't concern themselves with any spiritual activities at all but are just caught up in the world. Religious people also tend to form groups, and each group considers everyone else to be completely wrong. Tigers and wolves kill for food and don't eat vegetables, while rabbits eat grass. If a rabbit and a tiger tried to come to some agreement on how they could eat together, they could never reach any arrangement agreeable to both of them. This is why tigers and rabbits never try to come to this kind of an agreement—they always go their separate ways. This is the way people function in society; each person goes his own way and does what he wants to do. Trying to decide anything at all from a social standpoint is always absurd. Groups of people will always oppose each other on different points, and because of this there's no end to samsara. As social animals we all function like tigers and rabbits.

I would like to raise a point mentioned earlier—the same taste of pleasure and suffering. I'm very gross in my understanding and didn't quite understand how to put this into practice. I wasn't quite sure what to observe.

What one has to look for is the wisdom that is identical in both happiness and suffering—happiness no longer benefits, suffering no longer hurts, but one experiences the same taste of all phenomenal appearances. One ceases to make judgments and sees things as a single continuity without distinctions. Everything arises as the same taste.

What happens if one begins a practice that involves certain rules or precepts? Isn't there some conflict between this and practicing same taste?

Same taste is actually the only precept. In the Mahayana there are precepts such as not getting angry and not harming sentient beings. It is possible, however, to take a superficial approach to the matter. One can become preoccupied with the thought "There are sentient beings out there, and we must be careful not to harm them." But working from the basis of same taste, one realizes that there is no external reality, no internal self, nothing to choose between, such as suffering and happiness, or pain and pleasure. The concept of an external entity vanishes, and the precepts are thus kept naturally. The practice of same taste automatically brings about the keeping of all precepts.

You have suggested that we should always have our mind relaxed. I find—and I'm sure that this is true for all beginners—that certain situations are more beneficial for relaxing the mind than others. If we're in circumstances that are not conducive to relaxing the mind, it seems that either we practice same taste and thus try to use any situation to generate wisdom, or we find an environment that is conducive to relaxing the mind. There seems to be a conflict.

Never try to change your conditions—it is the practice of same taste that changes conditions. Don't go anywhere when you find yourself in unfavorable conditions, but practice same taste and this will create favorable conditions just where you are.

Does that mean that we should never try to go into retreat?

If you can really meditate and have a teacher who can indicate the nature of the mind in a manner you can understand, and if you can genuinely practice same taste, you need never go into retreat at all. You can do anything or go anywhere you want, because wherever you go and whatever you do is meditation. If you aren't really capable of meditating, going into retreat is like going to jail.

This seems to assume that we are all adepts at the practice of same taste rather than just having heard about it.

If you have heard about same taste and you haven't developed it, you have to do all the practices of the Dharma. You have to practice the Hinayana according to the Hinayana, the Mahayana according to the Mahayana, and the Vajrayana according to the Vajrayana. You have to take precepts and keep them, and you have to go into retreat and practice meditation.

You must have seen many images of deities, so you will have seen the skull cup filled with blood in the hands of the deities in the tantras. Kriya tantra is taught to beings who are very attached to cleanliness and purity. In this tantra, male and female deities are always separate and always have a simple and pure aesthetic form. There are also practices of wrathful or passionate deities that enable beings to train [their minds] by using their own aversion or desire. In the imagery of the inner tantras the deities are often shown in shocking positions. These deities never actually drink blood, eat excrement, or do many of the other things described in the tantras, but we who are trapped in erroneous conceptions of pure and impure can only relate to freedom from such conceptions through these images. These deities act in an outrageous fashion; the open expression of lovemaking, drinking blood, and eating excrement all point to the one taste of everything. The deities are described in this way in order to help us toward that realization; and when we make offerings to them, we offer not only all pure things but all impure things also.

I shall find it very difficult to come to terms with not realizing ultimate truth but receiving teachings about how to act from that state. Sometimes you seem to put a question from a relative standpoint and then answer in terms of ultimate truth. Relative and ultimate may be the same to a Buddha, but not to us.

Without the recognition of wisdom there's always dualizing, and when there is dualizing there is an outer world and an inner world. This leads to clinging to duality—that's samsara. The end one must work toward is the recognition of fundamental wisdom.

In the meantime, on the way to recognizing fundamental wisdom, how does one deal with the circumstances one lives in?

First we must make certain fundamental decisions: whether we prefer samsara or realization, and whether we want to get out of samsara. If we don't want to get out of samsara, there's really nothing further to consider. But if we decide that we do want to get out of samsara, we must then decide how to do it. We can approach this from the point of view of the Hinayana, in which case we have to take the precepts and engage in all the activities of the Hinayana. We can alternatively adopt the Mahayana point of view, in which case we have to develop the great qualities of the Mahayana. Or we can decide to enter the Vajrayana, in which case we have to receive the initiations, keep the precepts, practice the meditations, and so on, in order to attain primordial wisdom.

But at the same time we still have to make a decision. How do we do this without judgments?

It's not enough for me to decide to go somewhere solely on the basis of likes and dislikes; the proper criterion is which place will be beneficial. Having made a choice, I must live with it. If I decided I didn't like the place

I had chosen, I could move on, of course, but that might lead to constant dissatisfaction as I chose and rejected one place after another.

So you get stuck in one place?

First one examines different approaches to Dharma. This is like going to different places and seeing what work is to be had and what there is to do. Deciding to settle and take a job is like deciding to practice Dharma, and once this decision has been made, one has to abide by it and persevere to the end. If one decides to settle in Paris, for example, one must realize that this decision will determine the future course of events.

My question was whether it's better to take the decision to go to Paris and stick with it, or to wait until someone comes along and says, "Why don't you go to Paris?"

The important point is the initial choice. If we come to Dharma intending to practice, a judgmental attitude will not be helpful since it will raise a lot of obstacles to practice, but if we approach Dharma through its philosophy, we will need a critical faculty. Once the initial decision has been taken, we should follow it through consistently.

It seems that there should be some way to make judgments go with everyday life while still maintaining some sort of awareness of same taste, even at a very basic level. I don't think it's really necessary to create such a wide gap in terms of same taste between the enlightened being and the suffering samsaric person who is always wallowing in his dualistic nature.

Our volitional impulses are already judgments, and everything we do is based on judgments—there is no time when we are not judging, so the only opportunity for the practice of same taste is the moment of judgment. We already have such a glut of judgments that there is no need to make any more; we are trapped in the realms of samsara as a result of the judgments we have been making since beginningless time.

But if the three thinking processes are judgments, how do you stop thinking?

There is no need to obstruct conceptions at all, neither is it necessary to follow them. A good Lama will be able to indicate the nature of the mind, and you will understand why this is so.

Does one just watch the mind?

One has to watch the mind, but that is not enough. One must also seek the instruction of a compassionate Lama who has understood the nature of primordial wisdom. His indication of how to watch the mind will enable one to recognize wisdom, which is of prime importance in meditation. One should follow his instructions until one has developed confidence in the understanding of wisdom. Don't be in a hurry; trust Dharma. Don't be anxious that wisdom mind is a difficult thing to understand or that you are very far from understanding it. It can certainly be understood.

Westerners in general and Americans in particular sometimes create problems in their meditation by being in too much of a hurry. They want to do everything at once. This speedy approach only creates obstacles. One should not be in too much of a hurry to do anything. If one is speedy all the time, the mind gets scattered all over the place. If one takes a relaxed approach, the mind will be even and collected. Easterners are often very lazy, and for this reason they do not recognize the fundamental nature. Westerners are always in a hurry, and for this reason they don't recognize the fundamental nature either. Many Easterners may feel that they see the natural condition of mind in their own laziness; but although they may look very easygoing and relaxed, many of them have a lot of disturbance in their minds, though some do recognize the fundamental nature. Westerners have the problem that they tend to get battered by being speedy, so their minds aren't very collected or composed. Easterners don't have so many material possessions, so they can't get very involved in manipulating them. They tend to be lazy and become involved instead in their own minds, so the source of their laziness, and the source also of a lot of their Dharma practice, is basically much the same. Westerners generally have a very speedy, energetic approach to life, which they apply also to Dharma. They launch a grasping, energetic attack at Dharma with the feeling that it must be easy to attain realization, and so create trouble for themselves.

In general, people are prone to transfer to Dharma the attitudes of their day-to-day worldly habits. In the West a lot of thought and effort have gone into making life easy—push a button and things go on, push another and they go off. Things are made so that they are ready to function immediately. So people approach Dharma as if it, too, should be something easy, something similar to manipulating a material object. They approach

Dharma with their habitual speediness, grafting onto it their attitudes toward the material world. Dharma has nothing to do with one's attitudes toward the material world. Dharma has to do with working with one's mind and so requires a completely different attitude. If one takes a speedy approach to Dharma, one simply creates a lot of problems, but if one is open and relaxed about it, things become much easier.

3 · Nine Vehicles

Could you give some explanation of the view of Dzogchen?

If you want to learn about Dzogchen, you should find a good Lama rather than somebody like me.

Many of us are still trying to understand the doctrines of karma and rebirth. Could you say something about them?

There are many different systems of religious philosophy, both Buddhist and non-Buddhist, all of them intellectually created and intellectually expounded. From a Buddhist point of view, all philosophical systems fall into two general categories: eternalist and nihilist. Eternalist doctrines believe in some kind of god or gods who control events. If one believes in these gods, makes offerings to them, and follows their instructions, they will show favor, while if one omits these observances, they will be angered. Nihilism is based on the belief that there is no reality beyond that which is accessible to the senses, reality is no more than an aggregate of associated conditions, and when an appearance ceases, at death for example, total extinction has taken place, with no further result.

Buddhism does not agree with either of these extreme views. In Buddhist terms, mind is the source of everything. Mind is not objectifiable and has no reality that can be specifically indicated. If one recognizes the fundamental nature of mind, one is liberated, but if one becomes confused by the expression of mind and takes it to be something real, one falls into error, ignorance, and confusion and wanders in suffering. This mind, which has no reality of its own, is the source of everything—it is the source of samsara, the source of nirvana, the source of all thoughts and all appearances; it is the fundamental basis of everything.

There are many ways to describe the path as a whole, but in the Nyingma tradition we generally refer to the nine vehicles. These are Shravakayana and Pratyekabuddhayana, together constituting the Hinayana; Bodhisattvayana or Mahayana; the three outer tantras—Kriya, Charya, and Yoga; and the three inner tantras, Mahayoga, Anuyoga, and Atiyoga, or Dzogchen.

The Hinayana speaks of something called the individual mind. If this mind attributes a self to the individual, it has fallen into error, which brings about the conditions of suffering. Attributing a self to the individual leads to the creation of karma, which traps one in samsara. The phenomenal world is then taken to be something real. The fundamental Hinayana views, then, are based on the suffering and undesirability of samsara, and the lack of a real self in the individual. In order to realize these views, one must control and renounce the defilements and meditate on the repulsive aspects of samsara. The conduct appropriate to these views and practices is indicated by the ethical precepts: the refuge precepts, the precepts of a novice, monastic precepts, and so on. The fruition of the Hinayana is the attainment of the stage of Arhat. The word *arhat* means "one who has conquered all his enemies." "Enemy" in this context does not mean an external enemy but that which keeps us trapped in the realms of samsara.

In the Mahayana there are two different types of vehicles: the Hetuyana or vehicle of origin [vehicle of cause], and the Phalayana or vehicle of fruition [vehicle of result]. The basic quality of the Mahayana, as explained in many Mahayana scriptures, is that all sentient beings are in their fundamental nature and from the very beginning Buddhas, so potentially they can all attain full realization. Although all sentient beings are inherently Buddhas, Buddha nature is hidden by obscurations, but if these are purified, beings can actually attain Buddhahood.

The fundamental nature, or tathagatagarbha, is the source of the realization of all beings and inherent in all beings. Beings lack the appropriate conditions for the attainment of realization, however, but by relating to a realized individual, receiving teachings, and practicing Dharma, they can learn how to create these conditions. A seed cannot grow without moisture, warmth, fertilizer, and so on. Similarly, to attain realization based on the fundamental nature, the appropriate conditions are purification of the obscurations that conceal it.

One must understand the egolessness of the individual in order to recognize the tathagatagarbha as the fundamental source. The ignorant assumption of a self in the individual cuts one off from other expressions of the mind. These then appear to be objectified and other than the perceiving mind. Having isolated these seemingly external forms as something real, one creates a supposedly real world out of illusion. Constantly grasping at a self in particular appearances is an erroneous attitude referred to as grasping at a view of self in phenomena. Attachment to appearances then gives rise to the notion of an ego and to the defilements, since one attributes bad and good, harm and benefit, to external objects of grasping. In the Mahayana one must examine both oneself and the phenomenal world to discover the lack of any real self in either.

The basic distinction between Hinayana and Mahayana is that the former seeks to understand that there is no real self in the individual but does not seek to apply this to the phenomenal world. The phenomenal world seems to be the basis of experience, and the question is just left there without much further consideration. The Mahayana, on the other hand, seeks to establish the lack of real self in both the individual and the phenomenal world. The Buddha taught these different points of view to suit different attitudes. If one recognizes that there is no reality in the phenomenal world or in the individual, both the self and the world disappear as independently existent entities, and one becomes freed from samsara in accordance with the teachings of the Mahayana.

Although the Hinayana and Mahayana trainings are similar, their respective motivations differ. In the Hinayana one works basically to liberate oneself from the sufferings of samsara. In the Mahayana, however, one must work for the sake of all sentient beings—not only humans but also insects, other animals, and all the beings in other realms, such as the inhabitants of the hells and hungry spirits. Since the beginninglessness of all our lifetimes, all sentient beings have been our mothers. They gave birth to us, clothed us, and showed boundless kindness in bringing us up. The only suitable response to such kindness is the practice of Dharma and the attainment of realization for the benefit of all sentient beings. Worldly altruism with its relative framework doesn't have the force or strength of the practice of Dharma and cannot save beings from suffering in any permanent sense.

The Mahayana has the precepts of bodhichitta, which are the precepts of working for the benefit of all beings. There are many varieties of Bodhisattva attitude, contained in three types. The first of these is known as the king motivation. A king can work for the benefit of all his subjects, but first he must secure and maintain a position of power or he will have no basis for his activities. This is distinct from the Hinayana, in which one works only for oneself; with the king motivation one initially works for one's own realization so that one can benefit other sentient beings from that basis. The second is the boatman motivation. A boatman takes his passengers across the river with him—one thinks that practice benefits oneself and all sentient beings indiscriminately, like the boatman working equally for himself and his passengers. He may be the one guiding the boat, but the outcome is the same for him and everyone else. The third type is the shepherd motivation. The shepherd takes his sheep to pasture by herding them in front of him, keeping them on the path, and protecting them from predators and other dangers. The shepherd motivation is a high development of bodhichitta. One feels great concern that sentient beings should not be left in samsara, and works primarily for their benefit, ignoring one's own. Even if one is left alone in samsara, all sentient beings should attain realization. The motivation of such great beings as Manjushri and Avalokiteshvara is of this type. Although four types of motivation are sometimes mentioned, they can be summed up in terms of these three, and there is no difference between the sects regarding this teaching.

In the Mahayana the five paths and ten levels describe the same process of evolution toward Buddhahood. Briefly, the five paths of the Mahayana are as follows: The accumulation of merit and wisdom is the path of accumulation. Understanding the significance of the fundamental nature is the path of connection. Recognizing the fundamental nature is the path of seeing. Meditating on the fundamental nature is the path of meditation, and the path of no more learning is beyond all teachings. After traversing the ten levels and the five paths, one reaches Buddhahood, sometimes known as the eleventh level.

In the Phalayana, the vehicle of fruition, there are two divisions, the outer and inner tantras. The three outer tantras—Kriya, Charya, and Yoga—have basically the same approach, namely that one can purify obscurations by meditating on a particular deity and so directly recognize the wisdom nature of that deity. All the deities, whether male or female, are visualized separately. One adopts the attitude that the deity visualized in front of oneself is the supreme deity or the supreme form of that deity, like a king. Visualizing oneself as the deity, one imagines oneself as inferior, as if one were the deity's servant. One maintains cleanliness and a pure way of life, repeats the mantra, and makes many offerings to the deity. One does not offer meat or alcohol. The deities of the outer tantra wear very pure robes and jewelry, and never wear bones or go naked, unlike some inner tantra deities. It is said that the practice of an outer tantra leads to realization within a few lifetimes.

If one looks at a thangka, one can immediately see by some of the details whether it represents an outer or inner tantra. In outer tantra thangkas, the offerings will all be very clean and there will be no meat or gross forms of offering depicted. The deities will be single—even if a male and female deity are together, they will not be shown in union. To identify a thangka specifically, of course, one must consult the text.

Each outer tantra defines these principles more closely. In Kriya tantra the deity in front of one is seen as an expression of one's own pure mind. The relationship with the deity is one of equality, as with a brother or sister. Charya tantra resembles Kriya tantra closely in attitude, but lays an added emphasis on correct modes of conduct and elaborate offerings. The deity in front of one in Yoga tantra is also seen as an expression of one's own pure mind, but the inherent purity of the mind itself is given prominence, while the deity is seen as a subsidiary expression of that purity. According to tantric tradition these practices lead to realization in seven, five, and three lifetimes respectively. It makes no real difference which deity one practices, as they are all of the same nature, although they have different appearances.

The choice to practice a particular tantra depends on one's general attitude. People have different attitudes and capacities. Many Easterners are quite incapable of changing their modes of behavior. If one asked an average Indian to walk around this room naked, probably he would not be able to. If one asked a Westerner to do the same thing, quite possibly he would prepare to do so.

The inner tantras take a different approach. The basic view of Maha-yoga is that from the very beginning the fundamental nature has been the nature of the deities. We have never been separated from this nature, but obscurations have impeded its recognition; this is why we wander in samsara. The main emphasis is on the elaborate visualization practices of the development stage, leading to recognition of this nature. People often identify development-stage practice with visualization, although that is only one possible approach to it. Many people also have a lot of difficulty with visualization. They find it hard to imagine such great detail and to apply such a high degree of concentration. If people have little contact with their teacher, or if there are so many people around when they do see him that it's difficult to ask questions, they may not understand how to approach the development stage or hear of its different practices. If one approaches the development stage through visualization, one first does the preliminary practices and then receives from the Lama an initiation for a deity to which one feels connected. Then one learns the verses of the practice, performs the visualization, and repeats the mantra. Sometimes the Lama suggests the practice of a particular deity, sometimes a vision of a deity in a dream will indicate its practice, and sometimes one consults an oracle during an initiation by throwing a flower on the mandala: the section of the mandala on which the flower falls will determine the deity one should practice. When visualizing, one imagines one's body as the deity and as endowed with all its qualities. The form of the practice may vary from one sect to another, but the general principle remains the same in all sects.

One can also approach Mahayoga through what is called the profound development-stage practice of "spontaneous manifestation of appearance and emptiness." This is quite distinct from visualization. If one is not familiar with visualization practice, as is the case with Europeans, this is an excellent alternative. After one has received the initiation and teaching, the Lama will indicate how the nature of the mind is the nature of the deity. There are many Buddhas in the structure of the Three Kayas, but all are present as one's Lama, and by practicing in accordance with his instructions one can recognize how the Three Kayas are inherent in the mind. In this profound development-stage practice, one must first recognize fundamental awareness. It then becomes unnecessary to practice the complex visualization of the deities. Whatever appearances arise should not influence one. Whether one sees houses or trees, men or women, one should not be controlled by them or get wrapped up in them, but should always remain at the point of awareness.

People have different ideas about the location of the mind. Usually they think in terms of different parts of the body, but in fact the mind is nothing other than its own perceptions. It is incorrect to think that the mind is in the head or the heart, common misconceptions found in the West and the East. There is really no duality of self and other. If one allows the mind to remain in awareness, the distinction between the nature of the mind and its expression as phenomena vanishes. This is known as "the inseparability of appearances and emptiness." It is called a deity because the body as deity has no materiality and is beyond notions of good and bad—no benefit or harm can accrue to it. On the basis of this practice, the wisdom nature can arise as the expression of the deity. So when one hears a sound, one should not judge it but should remain at the point of awareness of the sound. A sound has no inherent quality of good or bad. If one does not discriminate between sounds but remains conscious of what is aware of them, one practices the same taste of all sounds. One will see that there is no meaning in any judgment or identification, and thus one will recognize emptiness. Remaining in that awareness, one performs what is called the practice of the speech of the Buddhas and recognizes the fundamental nature.

If someone accused me of theft and I reacted to his words as something real, I might become angry and perhaps argue with him, which would create a lot of bad karma and cause a lot of trouble for both of us. But if I recognized the words and the individual seeing them as simply my own projection and refrained from any judgment, I would leave them in the nature of same taste. Similarly, if someone were to praise me and I became attached to this, I might seek more praise, which would create more attachments and wanderings in samsara. If I recognized both the sound and the speaker as projections of my mind and left it at that, I would remain in the same taste. If one leaves sounds alone without making any dualizing judgments about them, they will remain in their own nature. That nature is emptiness, and that emptiness is the fundamental awareness. Recognizing emptiness through this practice of same taste is the recognition of Buddha nature through the nonduality of sounds. Applying the attitude of nondiscrimination to phenomenal appearances is the practice of the body of the Buddhas as the nonduality of forms. Circumstances and one's reactions to them may also become an object of this practice. In unfavorable conditions one may begin to worry, and as one becomes more involved with these conditions, more and more thoughts will be generated, creating a lot of karma. This may lead to insanity. On the other hand, becoming attached to good conditions and allowing oneself to be excited by them may cause pride, which also creates many different kinds of karma. Recognizing emptiness through awareness is the practice of the mind of the Buddhas.

There are many development-stage practices concerning each of the Three Kayas, but the practice I've been talking about involves all Three Kayas. The emptiness of appearances is the meditation on the Nirmanakaya, the emptiness of sounds is the meditation on the Sambhogakaya, and the emptiness of awareness is the meditation to realize the Dharmakaya. The profound development-stage practice of spontaneous manifestation of appearance and emptiness is a very easy but very subtle approach to the development stage, but since people are lazy it may be quite difficult for them to apply the practice.

In Mahayoga, the view is the mind as the nature of the deity, the meditation is the practice of same taste, and the conduct is avoiding discrimination. One eats any food whatever, bad or good, impure or pure, and acts without dualistic discrimination. In contrast to the outer tantras, in Mahayoga one does not give up meat or alcohol, but uses everything. Without the correct view, however, the conduct appropriate to this tantra cannot be expressed. When the correct view has been developed, the appropriate modes of conduct become possible. Without that view one might occasionally be capable of this conduct, but there will be no consistency to it since the mind is very unstable.

This teaching is in accordance with the tantras, and it should not be rejected as invalid. I've spoken about it in the hope that you will all be able to practice it one day and that hearing of it now will be of benefit, not with the idea that everyone can practice it immediately. Through study and the kindness of my teachers I know that this Mahayoga view is correct, but I don't have enough confidence to apply it myself. Once this view has been established, one can act out of the choiceless use of everything, but I have not developed this view to any extent. I can prove this quite simply. If some of the people here this evening encouraged me to make love to a woman in front of them, I wouldn't be able to do it because I'd be too embarrassed. This is a sign that I don't have the correct view. Alternatively, if there were some very unvirtuous person here who ought to be killed, I wouldn't be able to kill him because I don't have sufficient confidence in the correct view to undertake such activities.

In classical times, such great siddhas as Naropa and Tilopa in India and Milarepa and Drukpa Kunleg in Tibet seemed like madmen. They were generally held to be somewhat deranged, yet their seemingly mad activities were in fact an expression of their high development of this view. Drukpa Kunleg did everything he could to get his mother into bed with him. This is bad enough in most cultures, but in Tibet it's far worse because of the strong incest taboo among Tibetans. His mother was extremely alarmed, heaped abuse on him, and told him he was crazy, but Drukpa Kunleg continued in his efforts. Finally he promised faithfully that he would never tell anyone, and this convinced her. So he got her into bed—and then walked out on her. The next day he called a large group of people together and said to them, "If you try hard enough you can get people to do anything. If you really push it, you can even get your mother into bed—I know, I've tried."

A large number of other incidents concerning siddhas violating social norms are recorded in Tibetan literature. Such acts are not just erratic or arbitrary, but express the wisdom these siddhas had developed. It is very difficult to decide whether a person is a siddha, however. Some people who develop the right view are then able to adopt the crazy activities of a yogi, but ordinary people also may arbitrarily engage in these same activities. Some people can indulge in all manner of behavior. No matter how much they violate social norms by their sexual behavior, by drinking, stealing, or lying, they feel no remorse or shame. Such individuals' extremely straightforward conduct might make ordinary people mistake them for siddhas, while others might consider them frauds and denounce them. One should not form attitudes about this solely on the evidence of their conduct, but should try to determine whether their actions stem from pride or jealousy; if so, they do not have the correct view. Such a criterion is not totally infallible, however. Tilopa initially offered Naropa his female companion, then became very jealous and beat him up. This had nothing to do with personal jealousy; Tilopa was looking for a way to give Naropa a hard time in order to train him. The practice of Mahayoga can lead very quickly to recognition of the face and nature of the deity, but although many people practice Mahayoga, few are able to attain the Mahayoga view or develop confidence in it, so they do not gain the results of the practice.

In Anuyoga the main emphasis is on the completion stage, although there is also a development stage. There are two divisions of the completion stage in Anuyoga: Anuyoga with and without particular characteristics. The Anuyoga completion stage uses the nadis in the body, the prana or energy that moves through them, and the bindu contained in the prana. In such practices one must develop the view of basic space and wisdom, which is quite similar to the view of Atiyoga. Nowadays people do many kinds of physical exercise that also benefit the prana and nadis to a certain extent, but this physical benefit is only temporary. In Anuyoga one visualizes a large number of deities while at the same time performing the physical exercises and the respective mudras of these deities, thus training the body efficiently as well as developing the ultimate view. One creates the ultimate benefit of transmuting the body into the body of the deity as well as the temporary benefit of improving one's physical condition. Eventually one can attain realization by relying on the body through Anuyoga.

Dzogchen meditation is distinct from the Hinayana, the Mahayana, and any other tantra. In Dzogchen the natural condition of the mind is extremely important. Dzogchen has many different levels, but these can be divided into three sections concerning teachings on mind, teachings on the fundamental nature, and instructions. The precious instructions section deals with many methods, but the point underlying them all is recognition of one's awareness as [inseparable from] basic emptiness, and emptiness as fundamentally the Dharmakaya. In order to develop realization of the Sambhogakaya and Nirmanakaya aspects of the Dharmakaya, the practice of the natural expression of brilliant light is taught. The distinction between Dzogchen and all other vehicles is that Dzogchen is a far more effective approach for recognizing the true nature directly without going through many elaborate processes. This extreme directness is a great blessing. Although simple, it is nonetheless a profound teaching and supreme in its understanding. The practices and understanding of all other vehicles can be contained in Dzogchen, but no other vehicle can encompass Dzogchen. Dzogchen is a great teaching, but the individual must also be able to approach and relate to it. When this happens, the supreme circumstances for realization have occurred.

I've spoken a little about the structure of the vehicles and I've said a few words about some of the special characteristics of Dzogchen because I was particularly asked about them. But in some ways it is difficult to teach Dzogchen, particularly to a group. I don't hesitate to teach it in any sense, but there are some practical difficulties involved. First, there is the difficulty that I might be criticized by many Tibetans for teaching it to Westerners. This doesn't bother me at all, but nevertheless it would happen. Then, one does not usually teach Dzogchen without first examining each individual who is going to receive the teachings. One looks to see exactly what kind of people they are, what their minds are like, and teaches them accordingly. I don't like examining people, however. To examine people one has to look at them, find out what qualities and what faults they have, and formulate many concepts about them. This makes me too tired. I'm not personally acquainted with everyone here, and if I started talking about Dzogchen without examining people, it might turn out that some people are favorably inclined to the teaching and others are not. There might be Hindus in the room, there might be Muslims. There might be people here who like Dzogchen very much, and others who would be repelled when it is said that Dzogchen is the highest of all vehicles and would think I'm just talking too much, without discretion. If one approaches a Dzogchen master, however, it is quite likely that one will be able to receive the teachings individually.

Some people say it's essential to start the preliminary practices before you handle any teachings. Others say you must have a very firm background in the four reflections* or the graduated path.† What do you think about this, Rinpoche?

Both Buddha Shakyamuni and Nagarjuna emphasized the importance of gaining some intellectual understanding of Dharma before actually practicing meditation. This means listening to the teachings and reflecting on

---

*The four thoughts: blo ldog rnam bzhi.

†lam rim 'jug.

them, understanding the law of karma and the ultimate view, and recognizing the importance of Dharma. It is also very important to perform the preliminary practices, prostrations, and so on. The example is given of a man with no hands trying to climb a rock; he won't get very far. Similarly, if a person without any understanding of Dharma tries to meditate, he won't be able to get very far because he will have no clear idea of what he's doing.

The Buddha's teachings and the commentaries on them emphasize the importance of hearing and reflecting on the teachings and understanding their nature. However, hearing and reflecting on a few teachings without meditating on them is not only useless, but will even turn the teachings into a poison. This is worse than never having heard anything at all. The teachings of the Buddha cannot be rigidly defined, and his words often had many different meanings. He would often take one point of view in one situation and another in a different situation. In many cases he stressed the importance of hearing the teachings and reflecting and meditating on them. At other times he declared that to receive a teaching without meditating on it is to transform it into a poison that will destroy one.

It is necessary for each individual to discover his own relationship with the practice of Dharma. Meditation is extremely important, and many texts specifically concern meditation and clearly expound it. It is quite possible to enter Dharma solely through such texts. One can also approach Dharma through the specific meditation instructions that form the heart of the teachings. In this method it's not necessary to study very much. Another possible approach is the study of the central scriptures and the philosophical treatises. It is even possible to integrate some study of the central scriptures and philosophy with meditation practice, as I described earlier.

In Dharma and in Tibetan tradition, all fields of knowledge are assigned to five principal categories: art (including technical and manual skills), medicine, language studies, philosophy, and Dharma. The fifth is called literally "study for inner purposes" and consists of view, meditation, and conduct. Adding the traditional Indian studies of Sanskrit, poetry, metaphor, dance, and astrology gives the ten subjects.* Some Indian and

*Translated in other writings by Kyabje Thinley Norbu Rinpoche as art, medicine, language, logic and philosophy, and inner awareness, which are the five major fields of study, and poetry, semantics, composition, dance and drama, and astrology, which are the five minor sciences.

Tibetan teachers of the past mastered all these studies and skills, while some had only a very general grasp of them. Still others specialized in only one or two and developed complete mastery in their chosen fields.

Tibet originally had eight Dharma lineages, but these eventually crystalized as the four sects. A number of classical Tibetan scholars have classified the various lineages of Tibet into the tradition of scholarship, as developed in the Sakya and Gelug, and the tradition of meditation, as developed in the Kagyu and Nyingma. This description indicates general trends, but in specific cases there have been Lamas in all sects who mastered both learning and meditation. There have been learned scholars among the Kagyupas and the Nyingmapas, and great meditators among the Sakyapas and Gelugpas. Certain misconceptions are prevalent even today about the Gelugpas' concentration on ethical precepts and study at the expense of meditation. Such notions are not necessarily applicable. There are monks to be found in the meditative traditions and meditators to be found in the monastic traditions.

4 · Karma

The first thing to understand when approaching Dharma is the general nature of the world—why ordinary worldly existence is unsatisfactory and why it is essentially suffering. Then we should know what it means to attain realization. We should understand that there are specific reasons for working toward realization and particular benefits stemming from its attainment. Having understood these two points, the nature of samsara and the nature of realization, we don't really have to go very much further in learning about Dharma. We can proceed to meditate on that basis.

Please think for a moment and tell me if you really believe in the law of karma. Do you think it makes sense?

What's the law of karma?

"Karma" means processes. It means a cause like a seed and a result like a fruit. If you don't believe in the law of karma, I'd like to know, and I'd like to know why—please don't bother about what I will think. If you do believe in it, I'd like to hear your reasons for that, too.

What about agnostics?

Most sentient beings, cows for instance, take the agnostic attitude. But I want to know why people believe in the law of karma. How did the law of karma come about?

Do you believe in the law of karma?

Yes, I can't find any way not to. I don't really know exactly how it works, how to practice virtuous action and give up unvirtuous action, but I definitely feel it's true. I can't find any way out of the law of karma, and I feel

I have quite good reasons for believing in it. But giving up unvirtuous action and practicing virtue are not just theories; they must be expressed in our lives. Perhaps sometimes I can do this. But in particular instances, sometimes I can't tell what is virtuous and what isn't. In that sense I can't really say whether I know anything about karma or unvirtuous and virtuous action.

I think of karma as the law of cause and effect, and that's often demonstrated. If I go around with a frown on my face, people will avoid me, but if I look happy, people will be open and friendly. I don't have a problem accepting the law of karma for this life, but I do have a problem believing that I have accumulated karma in a past life. What I do believe is that life is all just a learning experience. Various difficult things happen to you, and you either go through them or you don't. If you don't, you have to face them again. Would you agree with this, Rinpoche?

It's very good to take the attitude that life is a learning experience. It's not uncommon for people to have difficulty believing that they have accumulated karma in a previous lifetime. This is partly due to the prevailing atmosphere of nihilism, which tends to reject the idea of any causal relationship that's not immediately perceptible. When a mentally slow or unstable child is born of mentally slow or unstable parents, Western scientific thinking might cite genes as the cause. I'm not suggesting that genetic theory is invalid; it certainly isn't contrary to the law of karma. However, the usual Buddhist view is that physical heredity is ultimately a result of karma. Therefore, if genetic combinations lead to a person's being born deformed or whole, with certain talents or abilities or without them, this is the product of his karma. Death in an airplane crash, however, obviously does not involve genetic factors. Airplane crashes are not hereditary.

There's not really a great deal to understand in karma, and although we can't hope to study everything in Dharma, karma is one thing that is useful to understand. Non-Buddhist philosophies fall into two types. Either they believe that all phenomena are the creation of an external god manipulating the world, or else they hold that everything is merely conditions without any interdependent structure, and that when a condition ceases it has no further result.

In the Buddhist view, the source of phenomena is the mind. It has no color or shape and no quality to which one can become attached; neither is it a nihilistic concept like empty space or non-existence. As a result of the initial lack of recognition of its own nature, the mind develops various habits. It creates a duality of an objectified realm and grasping mind, which leads to the notion of a self or ego. It then isolates factors of the objectified realm and develops various attitudes to them, bad and good, undesirable and desirable. Therefore, we are attracted by things toward which we have a positive attitude; we desire them and want to possess them. We are repelled by things toward which we have a negative attitude; we feel aversion toward them and want to push them away. Those things that neither attract nor repel tend to be ignored and fade from consciousness. In this structure, the three defilements of desire, aversion, and ignorance arise. Aversion gives rise to pride, and desire gives rise to jealousy, and in this way we become involved in the five defilements. More and more defilements stem from these five, resulting in the eighty-four thousand defilements. However, these are all present in a general sense in the five defilements, which in turn are contained in the three defilements. Ignorance is the source of the three defilements and so is really the worst.

Some scriptures say that desire is a great defilement and is the source of samsara, while others say the same of aversion. If we cannot give up the defilements as is taught in the Hinayana and if we cannot use the defilements as in the Vajrayana, they are all very dangerous. But all these defilements are rooted in ignorance. The root of the five defilements is not recognizing them, so in fact ignorance is the greatest defilement. Since olden times among Tibetans, those who keep their ethical precepts well often maintain that worldly people create the source of samsara in themselves through desire; whereas the worldly feel they are not doing anything wrong and accuse those who keep ethical precepts of being arrogant and prideful, which equally creates the source of samsara. We have all created a lot of karma through the process of objectifying an external realm and a subjective experience, grasping at various forms in that realm as good or bad, and developing attitudes of desire and aversion.

Since we have only two eyes and two ears and only perceive the physical world around us, it may be a little difficult to appreciate that we have been going through this process for millions of lifetimes. But perhaps if we consider this life, we may be able to form some idea of what previous lives have been like. If we look at people's physical characteristics, we find that some are tall and some are short, some are fat and some are thin, some are healthy and some are sick. Where do all these different conditions come from? One argument is that these physical characteristics are entirely due to genetic factors. Others say that it has to do with the nature of the locality in which a person is born and raised, and point out that people from hot countries are darker and people from cold countries paler. If such explanations were true, we would expect to find a much greater uniformity among people than we actually do. If we examine the mind, we find many different habits, often very marked. If these tendencies were inherited from parents or acquired through conditioning, children would always resemble their parents to some extent. But this is not necessarily the case. Very evil parents often have very good children, and good parents often have terrible children. There doesn't seem to be a direct relationship between parent and child in terms of mind, for the characteristics of mind are much too unique to have come from any particular hereditary factor. So where do they come from?

We might also consider the following argument formulated by Acharya Virya.* When a calf is born it already knows how to chew grass, and when a human child is born it already knows how to suck. Where do these tendencies come from? They do not seem to have their source in anything we can normally observe, so we might assume that they come from habits built up over many previous lives. Western thinking might suggest that the habit of sucking has something to do with the environment of the child in the womb. Yet another theory I have heard recently is that thumb sucking in humans precedes breast sucking, so breast sucking is the result of thumb sucking in the womb. However, these questions are rather cyclic. One might ask, "If breast sucking derives from sucking in the womb, where did the tendency to suck in the womb come from?" This merely adds another link to the cycle. It doesn't prove anything to say that breast sucking derives from some habit developed in the womb, because the habit developed in the womb must itself have a source. It's not at all

*Lopön Pawo, a great scholar who famously debated with the Indian master Aryadeva. He is also known as Aryasura, Ashvagosha, or Durdhasakala.

surprising that we find it hard to believe that we can experience the results of karma created in a previous life. Most people have this difficulty, since they have no experience of their previous lives.

Buddhism recognizes different types of karma according to how they come to fruition. Sometimes karma is created at an earlier stage in life and comes to fruition later in the same life. In other cases, enormous quantities of virtuous action may be created without coming to fruition in that lifetime. One might perform many virtuous actions, yet still experience nothing but bad luck and suffering and never enjoy much happiness. This is because a preponderance of unvirtuous karma created in previous lives obstructs the fruition of the virtuous action for this life. In such a case the virtuous action of this lifetime is not wasted, for in one or two lifetimes it will inevitably come to fruition. These are only two of the many ways in which karma ripens.

We should not be afraid of karma or think of it as totally negative. Karma is created entirely through our own volition: if our intentions are pure, we will create good karma leading to good results, but if we approach a situation with defiled intentions, we will create bad karma and experience bad results. So karma has both positive and negative aspects, and its creation depends entirely on our attitude.

One should avoid both the nihilistic attitude that everything is due merely to associated conditions and the mechanistic view that events and phenomena are brought about only by physical causes in a purely mechanical fashion. Karma is created by mind, expressed through mind, and worked out through mind—it is totally an activity of mind. Karma arises from grasping at duality, which in its turn comes from the notion of self. It was for this reason that Buddha Shakyamuni taught the lack of a self in the individual as an essential aspect of his doctrine. If we recognize that there is no real self, we will cease to create karma, and the cycle of confusion and suffering will come to a halt.

In order to annihilate karma completely, we must gain the insight into the lack of any real self, and in order to understand this, we must understand the fundamental nature of the mind. A Lama with insight can introduce the fundamental nature of the mind to us, and with this understanding we will be freed of any notion of a self and any tendency to attribute a self to any phenomenon. If we meditate on the fundamental nature of mind, the condition beyond any conception of self, we will cease to cling to duality, at least during meditation. There will no longer be any distinction between beings and realms, subject and object. These dualizing processes will all have disappeared, and karma, the result of grasping at dual conceptions, will also have disappeared. We can then forget about karma, because there is no more karma. We could forget about karma now, of course, but that wouldn't be of any use because we're still caught in grasping at duality. If we forgot about karma now we would continue to create it, and it could still be in force.

I'm confused about volition. Where does the volition to break out of the karmic structure come from?

First it's necessary to think. I spoke earlier about not making judgments and leaving the mind as it is. That state is beyond any kind of conception, but the initial understanding must inevitably come through metaphors and concepts. There are many ways of describing the principal characteristics of a human being, but the most basic quality is the ability to communicate and understand concepts. Emptiness is not empty like space but is essentially expressive, so the fundamentally pure nature of the mind is also essentially expressive. It is never obstructed but constantly expresses itself as manifest forms. Although we are only sentient beings, the essential brilliance of the fundamental nature is already expressed in us, and conceptions are among its expressions. If we leave the mind alone, it will remain in its own nature, and both impure and pure conceptions will be seen as just what they are. If we understand the fundamental nature, conceptions will disappear of themselves.

That's not really what I was getting at. It seems to me that there are two different levels of mind. There's the karmic level, full of obstructions and illusions, and there's a level of volition: at some point in your life, or in one of your past lives, some impulse made you follow the Buddhist path and appreciate the law of karma and ethics and so on. Where did that impulse come from?

We have a vast backlog of habits from previous lives, a few of which are being expressed now as the way we experience the world around us. There are many other kinds of habits that might cause us to experience it differently, but for one reason or another conditions may not be appropriate to the expression of these habits, so they lie dormant. We created all these habits in previous lives by creating different kinds of conceptions. We have created bad and good conceptions, impure and pure conceptions, each of which creates or reinforces a particular habit in us. At the moment, we are experiencing the expression of a certain set of habits, but these are not stable. Habits may suddenly arise and be expressed. Although these may appear to have no source, they come from a previous life, possibly even from many lifetimes ago.

The expression of a habit is dependent on conditions. In a previous life one might have created a habit inclining one to be virtuous. This might remain in one's character, but the conditions might not arise to bring it out. Suddenly one might find oneself in an environment where there are people practicing Dharma and trying to attain realization. This contact would provide the condition for that old habit to arise, and one would feel drawn to practicing Dharma. This can be compared to a piece of land on which there are many seeds. These seeds have the potential of growing into plants, but if the season isn't favorable, they don't grow. There are no conditions appropriate to their growth, so they just sit there. But with the change of the seasons and the coming of spring, it rains and the seeds begin to sprout. Fire provides another example. In Asia today, many villagers cook their evening meal over a wood fire. Then, instead of letting it die, they take the ashes and heap them up over the logs. The fire looks completely dead and even feels cool, but it's still hot underneath. In the morning they put some fresh wood on top, and it burns immediately. Although there's no perceptible fire, the potential is there in the ashes.

Ignorance is the worst of all the defilements. Ignorance has obscured the way mind functions and the way it expresses itself as the world. Because of this obscuration, we do not recognize past or future lives. We do not recognize the events that brought about particular results, and we do not understand karma. Ignorance, the worst of all defilements, has hidden this. But although we do not see its function, karma goes on. Once created, karma is never wasted but will inevitably come to fruition. Karma is like a bird and its shadow. A hawk hovering high in the sky does not recognize its own shadow on the ground below. Although that shadow is very distant, it will follow the bird wherever it goes, and eventually the bird will land exactly on its shadow. Once karma has been created, it will follow one like one's shadow, and when the right conditions occur, it will be expressed.

I have a problem with the Buddhist approach to reality, the teaching that the world is to be considered unreal simply because it's subject to constant change. In the West, of course, philosophers have always recognized that the phenomenal world is transient, but this has not prevented them from granting it a certain reality. What does Buddhism really say? Does it really teach that we should consider the phenomenal world as unreal? The second part of my question is this: if that really is the Buddhist teaching, what about cases such as Tibet before the Chinese invasion, when so many high Lamas were meditating on Buddhist philosophy and were nevertheless disturbed by the entrance of a solid and substantial army which didn't see reality in a Buddhist light?

Does the Chinese invasion in Tibet mean that the Chinese army is any more real than anything else? Consider the individuals involved—is a Chinese soldier any more real than a Tibetan? In the case of the Chinese army coming to Tibet, karma does not vary from its expression in any other situation. Based on ignorance, dual conceptions arise leading to the notion of a self. As a result of this dualizing self, people isolate phenomena as objectifiable and are either attracted or repelled by them. They create attitudes of aversion and desire with regard to these phenomena and so create karma. This produces the various conditions of experience. The Tibetan people created a lot of karma over a series of past lives through grasping at duality. This karma included a certain amount of merit, which kept the country peaceful for some time, but it was gradually exhausted, and other kinds, including unmeritorious karma, came to fruition. As a result they experienced events around them changing—the Chinese army came to Tibet. This was a result of the general karma field at that time.

That which arises in the field of wisdom has some kind of reality, but nothing arising in the field of ordinary mind has any reality at all. Since we don't understand its nature, it seems to be real, so we grasp at it. Everything is as real as we think it is. However, the reality we see in appearances does not exist; the reality that seems to be there is itself unreal. We can understand this just by examining the way the mind works. We might reflect on something we happen to like a lot, perhaps money, or a particular man or woman. Because the nature of phenomena is obscured by ignorance and defilement, we are attracted to this object or person and feel desire. If this desire is satisfied—if a man has a good relationship with a woman, for example—he feels happy at its fulfillment. Then if he loses the object of desire he will feel unhappy, and when he goes to sleep at night he will inevitably dream about the woman, or whatever the object of desire happened to be. With some meditation experience we might recognize that dream to be only a dream, but otherwise it will probably seem to be a real event. And because of the force of the propensities involved, we will act out all kinds of situations—maybe talk and be happy, maybe argue and feel sad, maybe make love, maybe break up again; something will happen in the dream as a result of the habits we had created, and it will certainly seem to be real. But how real is a dream? Dreams are made up of habits, and the waking state is also made up of habits. The body certainly seems to be real, it certainly has a lot of sensory experience, but it's just a bundle of propensities, a bundle of habits. As an example, there are a couple of cups of water here, and the way we relate to that water is governed by our conditioning. But we could try to think of it in a different way—as very sweet, for example. If we sat here repeating, "That water is very sweet, that water is very sweet," possibly we could convince ourselves, so that when we drank it, it would actually taste sweet.

In general, we tend to think that the waking state is more real than the dream state. One of the reasons for this is our familiar sense of time. When we are awake, it seems that the waking state lasts much longer than the sleeping state, and we conclude that it must be more real. But this is false. I might doze off for a moment and dream that I had gone to America. I might dream of building a house there, and not wake up until the building was finished. I might sleep for only a minute or so, and this would be the impression of the people around me as I slept, but in my dream consciousness I would have gone through a number of experiences requiring much more than a minute to complete. Duration of time is not a valid yardstick for any comparison between the waking and the dream state. Events and phenomena are just the result of a collection of habits. These habits are the source of all samsara, and they arise from grasping at the duality that comes from the notion of a self. Appearances are mere projections of consciousness. They have no objectifiable reality and are illusory and unreal, yet they certainly appear and function. This is called relative truth. However, relative truth is completely unstable and lacks the potential to be found in wisdom, the ultimate truth.

In the Hinayana, the understanding of lack of self in the individual is reached by considering the faults of samsara. One watches the mind and sees that human beings are just a bundle of flesh and bones, for example, or reflects that even chopping wood for a fire involves killing a few insects and inflicting suffering. Any desire causes suffering, and anything one might want is basically undesirable. Whoever might want it doesn't really exist in any case, since there is nothing to constitute an individual. There-fore, the Hinayana training aims at giving up attachment to samsara and gradually reducing the defilements by applying the appropriate antidote. The antidote to a man's desire for a woman, for instance, is reflecting on the repulsive nature of the organs and fluids inside her body.

The Mahayana teaches the recognition of the absence of isolated enti-ties. When regarding a seemingly external entity such as a woman, one takes the attitude that in reality there is nothing there, nothing that con-stitutes that entity. There is nothing that constitutes myself, nothing that constitutes a particular object in the field of perception—everything is merely illusion. By becoming absorbed in this way, one gives up unvir-tuous action.

In the Vajrayana the inner tantras teach that everything is an expres-sion of one's own mind. If that mind is impure, its expression will be impure, while a pure mind will express only purity. If the mind contin-ually watches itself and is not distorted into anything else, its natural, unobstructed expression and activity will be undefiled. Since the mind is originally pure, all its expressions, as in the example of a woman, are pure, and this recognition of the nature of mind leads to the experience of the wisdom of spontaneous awareness. The natural activity of the wisdom of spontaneous awareness is totally pure, and this wisdom expe-riences its own pure expressions. For a man experiencing spontaneous awareness, a woman is neither an object of renunciation nor something to ignore. We should not imagine that only women are to be purified, of course, or that only members of the opposite sex are completely pure and members of our own sex impure. All appearances should be seen indis-criminately as pure from the point of view of the wisdom of spontaneous awareness.

The many levels of Dharma teaching can be categorized as the Hinayana training, the Mahayana learning, and the Vajrayana precepts. The essence of the Hinayana training is weariness with the suffering and defilements of samsara; the essence of the Mahayana learning is the choiceless expression of benefit for all beings; and the essence of the Vajrayana precepts is the natural purity of all appearances. How we approach Dharma is entirely a question of individual choice. It doesn't matter to me what your approach is, and mine is my own concern. I don't know if it's possible to say that the Hinayana is a lower vehicle, the Mahayana a higher one, and the Vajrayana the highest of all three—the only meaningful sense in which one vehicle can be considered preferable to another is in its application to a particular individual. I do not feel able to keep all the precepts at all the levels. If I could even keep one type of precept, that would be very good, but I am not sure I would really be able to do so. I hope to be able to practice a little meditation, and I hope this will bring together all the precepts. Do you think this is possible? Do you think one could combine the hundreds of thousands of Vajrayana, Mahayana, and Hinayana precepts in one meditation? Can one even combine all the Hinayana precepts in one meditation?

As you said previously, the Hinayana is contained in the Mahayana, and the Mahayana in the Vajrayana, so they can presumably all be contained in some special meditation that gathers together all their moral attitudes.

It's much too difficult for me to put one thing into another and then into a third. There must be some meditation in which realization can be attained in one instant.

That's not what I meant—I didn't say we have to put one thing in another, but that they're all encompassed already in a fundamental attitude of mind.

How are they all contained in one meditation? How can all the Hinayana be contained in one moment of meditation?

All the precepts are based on emptiness and on trying to gain freedom from bondage, so if you realize emptiness and are free from bondage, all the precepts are present in your meditation at that instant.

That's very good, but how does that embrace Hinayana?

The Hinayana is intended to prevent the creation of new karma. This is particularly true of the vows of a monk. If a monk is meditating on emptiness and is free from samsara, then he's not creating any more karma, so all the precepts are contained in his meditation.

That's very good too, but how are the Mahayana precepts contained in the meditation?

The Mahayana is intended to liberate all sentient beings. If you're liberated, you show the path to liberation in that moment of meditation, emptiness, and liberation. Everything is contained in the mind, so if in my mind I'm not suffering, no one else is suffering. If I'm liberated, everyone else is liberated also.

You may be liberated in that moment, but what is happening to everybody else? The scar from my operation is very painful, and the people sitting here have sore knees. How has everyone become liberated?

That's only because they think they're not liberated. In one of the tantras it's said that even a dung worm is in bliss if it knows its own nature. If you know your own nature, you see everything as bliss and emptiness. Knowing your own nature keeps the Bodhisattva precepts. The tantra also says trying to save all sentient beings is a lie because it's impossible.

It's not good to mix up your systems. You've got to stick to one.

You were talking about putting all systems into one.

No, I wasn't—the question was about meditation.

Why isn't everybody liberated in that moment, then?

That's just what I'm asking you. According to what you say, they should be, but they're not. How can all the tantric precepts be contained in one moment of meditation?

My understanding is that the basic principle of tantric precepts is avoiding conceptualization. If one were free from conceptualizations in one instant of meditation, all the tantric precepts would be kept.

How can one be free of conceptualization? And who is going to be free of it, you or someone else?

What other ideas do you have about keeping all the precepts in one moment of meditation?

In the Diamond Sutra *it says that a Bodhisattva who conceives of sentient beings to liberate is not a true Bodhisattva. Since this is a Prajnaparamita teaching of the Mahayana, I would say that if the meditator is also free from conceptualization, he would meet the requirement in terms of the Mahayana.*

Are you referring to the part that says, "Whoever sees form and whoever hears sound does not recognize the true nature"?

That's also in the sutra, but in the part I was referring to, Shariputra tells the Buddha that the new Bodhisattvas are disturbed because they feel that it's impossible to save all sentient beings and at the same time practice the perfection of penetrating intuition. The Buddha explains that they should train their minds to avoid conceptions such as Buddhafields and sentient beings to be saved.

But that's clearly impossible. If one did not recognize something to begin with, how could one ever learn not to recognize it? There's nothing to be learned there.

What would you say is the essence of the tantric precepts, Rinpoche?

There are many, many tantric precepts, but the real essence of them all is pure perception. Unenlightened perception involves many experiences—water, glasses, tape recorders, people, walls, buildings, and all the perceptions of mundane consciousness—but the pure experience of all these phenomena is the perception of pure appearances.

You mean experiencing them just as they are, in a pure way?

Many meditations are taught in the tantras to lead to this experience. In the development stage, for example, experience is purified by visualizing one's surroundings as the Buddhafield, and all the people around as Dakas and Dakinis, male and female deities. I spoke earlier about the profound development-stage practice of spontaneous manifestation of appearance and emptiness, in which one watches one's own awareness in order to recognize the fundamental nature of the deity, which manifests essentially and primordially as the mandala. You've given me some good ideas, and now I'm going to try to describe how all the precepts are kept in one moment. In meditation, not necessarily Dzogchen meditation but meditation in general, one watches the fundamental nature of the mind, just as it is, without doing anything to it, without distorting it in any way. At the moment of recognition there is no subject of an individual and no object of a sphere or realm in which any subject could abide. Therefore, there is no object of samsara and no subject in samsara. At that moment one has become weary of samsara and given it up, and so one is a pure monk.

The fundamental nature has no independent reality, neither does anything else have any independent reality. There is no independent reality either in oneself or in anything else, and realizing this, one tends to become purposeless or aimless. There is no realm, no sentient being, and no purpose that any sentient being could ever have. Samsara is already empty, and since the emptying of samsara is the purpose of all sentient beings, the Mahayana precepts are kept.

If I were to drink this cup of coffee without attributing any reality to its taste, color, or form, it would remain in its own pure condition as the nature of the deity. This is in keeping with the Vajrayana precept of the pure appearance of everything, the fundamental awareness.

As long as we are externally oriented, dharmas are infinite. We can see this in the many different ways in which people approach their lives. There are Hindus, Buddhists, Christians, and Muslims. For some reasons Hindus don't like Muslims, and for other reasons Muslims don't like Hindus. Christians don't like Muslims or Hindus, while Buddhists are divided into a number of groups, some of which don't like one another. If we cease to be externally oriented, if we give up all dharmas and look at our own nature, there will be only one Dharma. I'm not really capable of practicing this, but I will pray that all of you will be capable of practicing the one Dharma. We can make obstacles for ourselves by trying to grasp at a lot of different teachings and undertake a lot of different practices; we can easily get caught in a collection process and fail to accomplish anything.

It seems that if the fundamental nature of mind is pure, and ignorance comes from defilements, then propensities must be very relative.

In the tantras the defilements are seen as mere momentary phenomena. There's nothing very serious in defilement at all.

Then karma and habits are very relative?

Yes, karma is only relative. But as long as we are caught in grasping at duality, we continue to function within karma, and as long as we remain within that framework, we must give up unvirtuous action and practice virtuous action. If we maintain an open mind about our practice, an external observer will probably think that we are forgetting or dropping certain parts of it, but in fact we will really be developing in Dharma. Whatever practices fall away will just be a factor of our development. After all, Dharma is not something to be materialized as necessary or valuable in itself; it is only a means. If we want to go from the U.S. mainland to Hawaii, we must find some kind of means of getting there. Similarly, in striving to free ourselves from samsara and attain realization, we must use some kind of means, so we take up the practice of Dharma. When the ship or plane reaches Hawaii, we automatically get off. When we reach the ultimate realization through practicing Dharma, it is not even necessary to give up Dharma—it will disappear by itself.

The greatest enemy of Dharma is doubt. When we set out to practice Dharma, we must develop the determination to follow through with it, to persevere in the development of realization. In Tibetan Buddhism there are many symbolic portrayals of male and female figures in union, and many Tibetans who practice Dharma feel that these symbolic expressions are just something to meditate on, with no indication as to any further practice. These people make judgments and decisions. But Dharma is not just symbols; it's also something significant and real that we have to practice. If we are going to practice in any real sense, we should avoid doubts and not worry about anyone else's opinion. We should just practice straightforwardly to attain realization. In the symbolism of male-female union, the deities are not joined in mundane desire but as a means to control and destroy the defilement of desire. It is their desire itself that achieves this, a desire beyond the realm of ordinary desire. This is not the union of ordinary beings. The female figure represents essential emptiness, and the male figure represents phenomenal expression. Their union represents the inseparability of phenomenal expression and essential emptiness. All the symbolism of the various deities is a means of training and subduing the defilements—they are in fact antidotes.

5 · Buddhahood

Over lunch yesterday I mentioned that just avoiding bad and trying to be good seemed very compulsive, and didn't seem to get to the root of the matter. You said that as long as we're not enlightened, we must have some guide, something to work with. In final enlightenment and wisdom there is no longer any practice of virtue or avoidance of nonvirtue, but until we reach that point, we need some practice to work with. It seems to me that the practice of virtue becomes dualistic and that there should be some other, nondualistic way of working with this problem. I gather we can use our nonvirtuous activity as a means to see emptiness?

Our discussion yesterday was initially about meditation. We began by distinguishing between conceptual and nonconceptual virtuous action. Nonconceptual virtuous action is the practice of meditation and the recognition of wisdom; there is no need for virtuous action of body and speech, or any need to repeat any mantras or sutras while sitting and recognizing the fundamental nature. However, we are not always practicing meditation. We are often involved in activities of one sort or another, and it is necessary to utilize conceptual virtuous action in order to continue the practice of the path at those times also. If we tried to practice conceptual virtuous action while meditating, the force of conceptuality would counteract the meditation and we would feel great despair from this conflict. But when involved in ordinary activities, we are under the influence of grasping at duality, so it becomes important to use the appropriate means, the conceptual modes of virtuous activity.

Do you remember what I was saying about habits?

I think you said that until we're able to eliminate all habits, there is a need for a conceptual framework of virtuous action. Then we had some discussion about whether the extinction of habits in Buddhahood implies that for a Buddha there is no longer any hunger or thirst or any other need. Then we discussed whether the activity of compassion was a habit. We finally decided that it would be a contradiction to consider compassion to be a habit, since compassion is absolute emptiness. If compassion were the result of habits, it wouldn't be true compassion.

Habits come from grasping. A Buddha is altogether free of habits, but we ordinary sentient beings have negative habits that keep us trapped in samsara. In seeking liberation from samsara, first it's necessary to work with these habits and purify them. Then, as we work through the various levels of Bodhisattvahood—the ten bhumis, or levels—habits are gradually eliminated, until at the tenth bhumi they have become very subtle. When Buddhahood is attained, they vanish altogether, because grasping at reality and illusion has ceased. Ignorance is replaced by the wisdom of Buddhahood, and since no grasping arises from wisdom, it follows that a Buddha has no habits. In other words, when we start on the Bodhisattva path, negative habits are gradually replaced by positive ones and are eventually eliminated through the reduction of grasping, until in Buddhahood there are no habits whatsoever.

Do you think a Buddha sees all the realms of all sentient beings? According to some traditions, a Buddha sees all the realms of all sentient beings and is able to benefit them by manifesting as various enlightened beings and teaching the Dharma. If he did not perceive all realms, how would he be able to benefit sentient beings?

Who is it that sees? Shakyamuni is dead; he can't see anything.

The body of Buddha Shakyamuni certainly expired. But if Buddha Shakyamuni died, he was just an ordinary sentient being. What good would he be to us, then?

He told us about emptiness.

Who did he teach emptiness to?

Us.

Did he benefit us or not? There are uncountable numbers of Buddhas, though they can all be said to be contained in Buddha Shakyamuni. How can a Buddha benefit sentient beings? Does he recognize the realms of sentient beings or not? What is the basis for the arising of his compassion? Where did it come from if it arose spontaneously?

According to the teachings of Jigme Lingpa, a Buddha perceives his own voice as an echo. He does not perceive himself as acting compassionately, but an external observer will perceive him as giving teachings and initiations.

If a Buddha does not perceive himself as giving teachings although sentient beings perceive these teachings being given, how does the connection between a Buddha and a sentient being occur?

Karma?

Can all sentient beings hear the Dharma?

If they're not deaf.

Did you ever hear a sound in your dreams? Did you have ears at that time? If so, were they the ears you have now or different ears? If they were the same ears, you weren't asleep.

Was there ever any sameness from one moment to another?

If it seems to you to be the same, then it's the same. If not, it's not the same—everything is just what it seems to be, and nothing ever occurs except as an expression of habits. From beginningless samsara we have been creating all kinds of habits, which go on and on finding their own expression. Even our own body is not objectifiably real. It's just an expression of the propensities we have built up and only seems to be there because of our habitual reference to it. Other than that, it has no reality. Things are only what they seem to be.

You come from Honolulu. When you think of home, has your mind gone from Kathmandu to Honolulu? Can you remember what's lying beside the telephone in your house?

In a dream, I can remember.

These memories come from habits. Hearing Dharma from a Buddha is an expression of our own field of habits, and hearing or experiencing bad things is an expression of our own negative habits. Both these types of habit have been built up over countless lifetimes.

In the Hinayana, a Buddha is traditionally defined as having defeated and transcended the defilements, and an ordinary sentient being is defined as being under the control of the defilements and subject to grasping. Such an individual is involved in the arbitrariness of his own projections—something like our own condition. By overcoming the defilements, an individual transcends samsara and attains realization. According to the Mahayana tradition, a Buddha first develops the motivation to save all sentient beings from suffering and then accumulates merit and wisdom for countless eons. Finally he attains the full realization of Buddhahood, described in the Mahayana sutras in terms of the Three Kayas: Dharmakaya, Sambhogakaya, and Nirmanakaya.

Although ordinary sentient beings are not actual Buddhas, they all have Buddha nature, the sugatagarbha. Before attaining enlightenment, the Buddha also had this Buddha nature, and in front of a great number of spiritual friends he prayed that he would attain realization for the sake of all sentient beings. Taking many births as a Bodhisattva in many different forms, as both men and women, he acted for the benefit of beings in different ways and so finally attained full realization. This was the realization of the Dharmakaya.

In the Dharmakaya there is no grasping whatsoever, so there is no entity that can be indicated. The Sambhogakaya abides as the expression of the Buddhafield and is itself inseparable from the Dharmakaya. In the general tradition it is said that it is the Nirmanakaya aspect of Buddhahood that works for all sentient beings. According to the Nyingma tradition, however, the Buddha went through a great many lifetimes as a Bodhisattva, creating pure prayers of aspiration for all sentient beings. This is the expression of a Buddha as Nirmanakaya working for all sentient beings.

Working for all sentient beings is a result of the prayers of aspiration that the aspirant to Buddhahood made on the path. It is not a result of any grasping on the part of the Dharmakaya, because the Dharmakaya has no grasping and does not conceive of any duality of Buddha and sentient beings. Nonetheless, the appearance of a Buddha giving teachings occurs. This is like the reflection of the sun and the moon in a pool of water. The sun and the moon have no intention to enter the water, but as long as the water is clear, the sun and moon will be reflected in it, and there will be as many suns and moons as bodies of water. If the water is not clear, the sun or moon will not be reflected in it. In the same way, the manifestation of the Nirmanakaya occurs as a result of the prayers of aspiration of Bodhisattvas on the path, together with the fundamental sources of tathagatagarbha inherent in all sentient beings. Buddhas do not in any sense leave their enlightenment in order to express the Nirmanakaya in the ordinary world, just as the sun and the moon shining in the sky do not leave their places in order to be reflected in the water. Since the tathagatagarbha, like clear water, is always in the appropriate state, the mind can become clear in association with a pure Lama. As a result of association with the Nirmanakaya, sentient beings are drawn to take refuge, develop bodhichitta, give up unvirtuous action, and practice virtuous action. Leading beings to these acts is an aspect of Buddha activity. The Nirmanakaya expresses itself in countless ways—as officials, hunters, prostitutes, teachers, virtually any kind of person. Buddhahood does not express itself only as Lamas or religious instructors.

What I have been describing so far is the Nyingma Sutra tradition, but in other traditions it is said that a Bodhisattva works ceaselessly on the path to realization. Having attained Buddhahood, he does not simply remain in his enlightened condition but works for the sake of all sentient beings, perceiving them and their realms. The Nyingma tradition has no objection to this viewpoint. The Nyingma viewpoint is based on this reasoning: if, after attaining realization, a Buddha were to perceive the realms of sentient beings and were to create manifestations for their sake, that Buddha would be clinging to a realm, clinging to a conception. If he clung to a conception, he would not be a Buddha. In the Nyingma tradition it is said that a Buddha has no clinging and consequently perceives neither sentient beings nor their realms. What is referred to as the Nirmanakaya benefiting all sentient beings is a manifestation of his aspirations for all sentient beings. These aspirations were born when he was a Bodhisattva and brought to fruition by the fundamental source, tathagatagarbha, and association with a spiritual friend. This brings about the manifestation of Buddhas in the world.

In general, the three New Translation sects (Kagyu, Sakya, and Gelug) hold the former opinion, while the Nyingma holds the view that I have just described, but this is not an absolutely fixed rule. A number of people in the New Translation sects approach the Nyingma view, and a few Nyingmapas, especially scholars, come close to the view of the other sects. According to your karma and your feelings about the question, you can take whatever viewpoint you think best, but I thought it might be of benefit for you to hear about these alternative opinions. Perhaps this will help you in approaching further study of the matter.

If we saw a Buddha performing specific acts, we might think he was involved in discrimination. If he were brushing his teeth, he would appear to have the idea of teeth, toothbrush, and so on. If we did see a Buddha brushing his teeth, would it be only our own habits that made us see this? Presumably he would not see himself as brushing his teeth.

That's correct. That is the meaning of saying that no Buddha ever teaches anything. It's only in the perception of a sentient being that anything is taught. A Buddha has no grasping, so there is no perception of realms, sentient beings, and the act of teaching; but as a result of karmic connections, sentient beings perceive a Buddha and experience him as teaching. Even though it might appear to an ordinary being that a Buddha had some grasping, as in the toothbrushing example, from a Buddha's point of view there is no grasping at all.

As long as we are involved in habits and grasping at duality, we must have faith in the Buddha and persevere with our meditation. It's very important to understand this thoroughly. If we took a simplistic attitude to this teaching, we might then believe that a Buddha is merely a manifestation of our own mind and that there is no reality in a Buddha. This could easily lead people to abandon the Buddha and the Dharma, and I would fall under heavy criticism. Not that I mind heavy criticism, but I do mind people abandoning the Dharma.

I've made a few distinctions with regard to sects here, but one can't make any hard and fast generalizations about any sect. There are different opinions and ideas in all sects, as well as bad and good people, and bad and good qualities. One shouldn't make too much of sectarian distinctions. As far as the two views of a Buddha's enlightenment are concerned, no strict distinctions can be made on a sectarian basis, for different views are held in all traditions.

The description of the Three Kayas found in the Nyingma tantras differs again from the Sutra tradition. To recapitulate, according to the Sutra tradition, the tathagatagarbha, which is inherent in all sentient beings, is the fundamental source of the Nirmanakaya, while the prayers of aspiration of a Bodhisattva on the path to Buddhahood and his accumulation of merit and wisdom are the contributing circumstances. According to the highest Nyingma tantras, the Buddha was never deluded. From the very beginning of beginninglessness, he is already realized and recognizes his own realization. This is referred to as the Buddha Samantabhadra, who always was and always has been enlightenment itself.

Samantabhadra is the Dharmakaya aspect of realization, which can be described in terms of the two purities, the essentially and primordially pure Buddha nature, and the freedom from sudden stains in pure Buddhahood. The first of these purities, the essentially and primordially pure Buddha nature, is already present in us. If our own nature were not essential primordial purity, there would be no way ever to attain realization, so what we must do is recognize this purity. This raises the obvious question, "We aren't Buddhas, we're sentient beings. How did we get into this mess if we're essentially and primordially pure?" The reason is obscuration through what are called sudden stains, freedom from which is the second purity. These sudden stains are the errors of grasping at a dual structure of objectified realm and subjective inhabitant, and it is through not recognizing the essential primordial purity that we have fallen into this error. We develop the notion of an ego, we develop habits, we develop clinging to a self, we develop the structure of a realm and an inhabitant, and in this way the essential primordial purity is obscured. Samantabhadra has never fallen into this error. He has always recognized his own essential and primordial purity and has always remained in immutable Buddhahood. If we recognize the essential and primordial purity, these sudden stains that come from error will disappear and we will realize the two purities of Buddhahood.

What is meant by the word "sudden" here?

The Tibetan word is *lobur,* meaning "sudden" or "temporary," and the sense can be illustrated with the example of a cloud. A cloud has no real substantiality; it can of course be explained in terms of moisture rising through heat and condensing due to the coolness of the upper atmosphere, but a cloud is only something that occurs due to particular conditions, and under different conditions it disappears again.

But isn't everything like that?

The Hinayana and Mahayana don't concern themselves with sudden stains,* since a different level of understanding is involved. Doctors don't practice law, and lawyers don't practice medicine; in the same way we should never mix different levels of understanding. But in the Nyingma tradition of Vajrayana, all of samsara is a sudden stain; *lobur*—"sudden" or "temporary"—is the opposite of "permanent." The defilements are an example. If we saw a beautiful woman we might feel attracted to her, or if we saw an enemy we might feel aversion toward him. These feelings occur where they weren't evident before and are subject to change. But they're not permanent. We may feel attracted to a beautiful woman, yet suddenly find ourselves hating her. And strong hate for an enemy may change to affection.

If these things are temporary, what's permanent?

The only thing that can be said to be permanent is that which does not conceive of either permanence or impermanence—the Dharmakaya. However, one can't decide there is only one way to see this. The third Karmapa, Rangjung Dorje, described three things as permanent: the Dharmakaya is permanent in its essential quality, the Sambhogakaya is permanent in its continuous flow, and the Nirmanakaya is permanent in its utter uncertainty.

According to Longchen Rabjam, however, the Dharmakaya is beyond both permanence and impermanence. Although this may seem completely opposed to the teaching of Rangjung Dorje, it merely reflects a different emphasis. Calling the Dharmakaya essentially permanent refers to its unchangingness, which does not contradict the assertion that it is beyond both permanence and impermanence; Karmapa Rangjung Dorje was not attributing any essential, permanent "thingness" to the Dharmakaya.

*glo bur gyi dri ma (phonetic spelling, *lobur gyi trima*).

The two purities that constitute the Dharmakaya express themselves as brilliant light, which contains in itself all the kayas and wisdoms of the Buddhas. Unlike sentient beings, a Buddha has no habits, but his Dharmakaya nature expresses itself as the brilliant light that is the Sambhogakaya. Although two purities are also attributed to the Sambhogakaya, these are not different from the two purities of the Dharmakaya. The Dharmakaya of the two purities expresses the brilliant light, and the brilliant light is in itself the Dharmakaya of the two purities—these two are not distinct. These two essentially inseparable aspects are naturally unobstructed and beyond all conception. This unobstructed aspect of the Dharmakaya and the Sambhogakaya together is the expression of the compassion of Buddhahood, and the foundation of the Nirmanakaya. This is sometimes referred to by writers other than Longchen Rabjam as compassion itself, but Longchen Rabjam described unobstructedness as the basis of compassion; based on this unobstructedness, anything at all can arise, effortlessly manifesting for the benefit of all beings.

The Nirmanakaya has no aim or purpose. It does not try to do anything, but wherever there are sentient beings it manifests itself as the natural expression of enlightenment, the compassion of the Buddha, without habits, conceptions, or purpose.

I've described the Three Kayas in accordance with three traditions—the general Buddhist tradition, the specifically Nyingma tradition of the sutras, and the tradition of the highest Nyingma tantras. Please don't get them confused. One should not, of course, imagine that there are separate Nyingma sutras. All the sutras were translated in the Nyingma period, principally by the Great Translator Vairochana. These sutras were widely studied in Tibet, and various learned men wrote commentaries on them according to their understanding. These scholars took slightly different positions on the meaning of the sutras, and so the varying views concerning the Sutra teaching of the Three Kayas arose. If several students of a learned teacher compare notes after his lecture, they may have somewhat different ideas on the exact meaning of what he said, even though they may all feel that they have understood him correctly. Similarly, slightly different opinions arose concerning the Sutra teaching on the Three Kayas, although no such differences are found in the scriptures themselves.

When studying the Dharma, try to keep a very open mind, and then contemplate it. There is a lot to know even about one single word. For example, *shunyata,* or "emptiness," is a single word. In the Hinayana [sutras], *shunyata* refers to the lack of a personal ego. From the Mahayana point of view,* it means the essentially empty quality of everything, while in other [Mahayana] sutras,† it means the brilliant light nature. In Dzogchen it means the primordially pure nature. *Shunyata* has different meanings on different levels. We cannot have one fixed idea about anything, for different meanings apply in different contexts.

The basic difference between the Hinayana and the Mahayana is the latter's acceptance of the tathagatagarbha; there is no concept of tathagatagarbha in the Hinayana. The Hinayana does not accept the Sambhogakaya either. Altogether there are seven Mahayana views that the Hinayana does not accept. For example, in the Hinayana it is not considered virtuous to prostrate to Tara, since she is female. We should not form negative opinions about these differences, but it is important to understand them.

In the Hinayana, the mind is considered to be just an ordinary state, inseparable from the defilements, whereas the Mahayana speaks of the fundamental source of Buddha nature, the tathagatagarbha or sugatagarbha, inherent in all beings. In the inner tantras, the mind is seen as always having been the nature of the deity. The highest tantras‡ hold that the fundamental nature has been enlightened from the very beginning, but sudden stains have temporarily obscured it, so one must apply the appropriate antidote in order to clear away these obscurations and attain ultimate realization.

Some people seem to feel that studying is not particularly useful in Dharma and is just another source of error. Others feel the same way about visualization and the repetition of mantras, and think meditation is the most important. But we should not disparage different approaches to Dharma. Study can help us understand unvirtuous and virtuous action and the nature of samsara, and with that understanding we can begin to

*Taught during Buddha's second cycle of teachings, mainly revealing shunyata.

†From the third cycle of Buddha's teachings, about tathagatagarbha.

‡Here, "highest tantras" refers to the tantras of Dzogchen, particularly upadesha or the precious teachings section, Dzogchen mengak (rdzogs chen man ngag).

approach the ultimate nature. It is said that words are metaphors. Without metaphors it is not possible to get at the meaning; similarly, without approaching the ordinary world we cannot get at the ultimate nature. Both study and mantra repetition are designed to help beings attain realization, and there is no reason to discourage others from these approaches to the path even if we have no aspiration toward them ourselves.

Some people even say that development-stage meditation is just mental projection with no reality and that it just builds difficulties. But this is not the case. Development-stage practice is absolutely necessary. In the ordinary human condition we experience many impure and pure things that seem to be bad and good. I happen to like things clean, and I got used to this when I was in the West, where the cities are rather cleaner than they are here. When I returned to Kathmandu, things seemed a lot more mucky, and when I was walking along the road I would notice a lot of shit. If I felt repelled by this and kept creating a duality of clean and unclean in my mind, I would reinforce the tendency to grasp at duality. If I accepted the dirtiness, feeling that clean and unclean are just my own karma and that it does not make much difference what one experiences, I would gradually wear away this grasping at duality. Development-stage practice is intended to help us learn and understand the experience of purity. When we hear a sound, we will either become attached to it or feel repelled by it; we will be involved in duality in terms of sounds. In the development stage we meditate on deities in order to experience all worldly phenomena as the pure mandala of deities. Forms become the forms of the deities, sounds become mantras, and conceptions become the nature of wisdom.

This is in accord with most tantras, but in Dzogchen the approach is different. Although sometimes taught in connection with visualization, the Dzogchen view is quite distinct from the visualization practices. In Dzogchen, visualization is not considered the main aspect of practice, and one does not necessarily have to practice visualization at all. In Mahayoga, the main practice is visualization, and in Anuyoga the main practices are visualization and control of the nadi, prana, and bindu by means of various exercises. In Dzogchen, it is said that one does not really have time for all these activities. The actual Dzogchen practice is recognizing the fundamental nature, the ultimate view. Having recognized the fundamental nature, one must continue to meditate on it without doing a great number of other things. This is the essential quality of all meditation. Doing many different Dharma practices is also good, but somewhat less to the point. It is very good to give up unvirtuous action, and it is always better to perform a virtuous action than an unvirtuous one. There is no need ever to perform an unvirtuous action, but on the other hand there is no need to go around trying to accumulate virtuous actions. If there are black clouds in the sky, the sun will be obscured, and if the clouds are white, it will still be obscured. Whatever activities one tries to do will obscure things—shackles are still shackles whether they are iron or golden, and whether obscurations are pleasant or not, they are still obscurations. The essential quality of Dzogchen meditation is the recognition of the fundamental nature. Other Dharma practices may be good, and may be preferable to things one might otherwise become involved in, but they are less direct.

If we follow a Lama who has wisdom mind, he will be able to introduce the fundamental nature without using any concepts, and without our having to think about it or become involved in any idea of it as anything at all. We will experience it directly. Without any concept at all, we will understand the Dzogchen view. It is not enough just to have the idea of Dzogchen as a practice without bad or good, without unvirtuous or virtuous action, and leave it at that without going any further.

There are two levels in Dzogchen. The first teaches how to understand and realize the Dharmakaya, and the second teaches how to realize the Sambhogakaya and Nirmanakaya. Concerning the Dharmakaya, we already have the essential and primordial purity but have not developed the freedom from sudden stains. The purpose of meditation is to free ourselves from sudden stains. These practices are not complex—recognize the fundamental nature and meditate on it. There is really little else to do if we follow a good Lama.

I am not a great Lama, and there is not much I can say about Dzogchen to help you understand it in greater depth. In a sense Dzogchen is a very difficult subject to talk about. There is the Dzogchen account of a perfect woman, for example, with a description of her waist, her hair, and so on. If I were to start talking about these things, it would arouse a lot of jealousy.

A Dharma teacher would normally approach teaching in this way: first he would develop bodhichitta, then he would give the teachings themselves, and finally he would distribute the merit to all beings. In this situation, however, I do not consider myself a Lama, so I have not adopted that approach. I have come here as a friend just to talk with you. Nevertheless, I have tried to give due thought to what we have been discussing and to talk in accord with Dharma. I have sometimes joked and sometimes been a little abrasive, and if I were trying to teach anything, this would definitely not be in harmony with the way Dharma should be taught. But I feel that such approaches are sometimes necessary to help people understand Dharma, and I have not adopted them without good reason.

We should pray that our activities here in Nepal will benefit all beings, especially our friends in the West. Dharma has been spread to a certain extent in the West, yet there is a good deal of sectarianism and misunderstanding there. When hearing Dharma, we should pray that all beings will understand it appropriately—this constitutes the distribution of merit and the prayer for all beings.

At the moment of absorption in the Dharmakaya, when you're free of sudden stains, are you necessarily in a state of evenness?

When one realizes the fundamental nature, everything abides evenly. But if one thinks everything is in evenness, then it's not, and one has failed to understand.

Is there a catalyst or something that triggers these sudden stains?

The sudden stains occur through failure to recognize fundamental awareness.

What's the cause of that?

The cause of failing to recognize basic awareness is ignorance, but ignorance can be used. If one follows a Lama and learns to apply the methods skillfully, ignorance itself can be used in order to recognize awareness. It is very important to find a compassionate Lama who understands the nature of wisdom and has a high degree of insight. Such a teacher will be very skillful. A teacher without insight may have a certain amount of understanding, but he will not be able to benefit people very much. He may teach

Hinayana when Mahayana would be more appropriate. Some teachers with great learning but little insight teach only one level to everybody, and some do not know how to bring a particular individual from a lower level to a higher one. The disciple may already have reached some understanding of the fundamental nature, and if he communicates his understanding to a teacher who has real insight, that teacher will immediately recognize it and be able to increase the disciple's understanding. If the teacher is basically just an intellectual, however, he will be unable to understand where his disciple is and so will fail to increase the disciple's insight. His intellectual approach may produce confusion; he may say that there is something wrong with his disciple's insight and take him away from it.

If we are so lost in ignorance, how can we decide if the Lama has insight? How can we perceive whether he has the right view of us?

This is the very reason why the scriptures talk about the need to create good karma and make a lot of prayers of aspiration.

You defined the Sambhogakaya as brilliant light, but in the sutras it's generally defined in terms of place, time, teacher, retinue, and teaching. These seem to be two completely different things.

Those five factors concern the structure and form of the Sambhogakaya. Brilliant light is the source or nature of the Sambhogakaya. These two are not different. But I am only a sentient being with an exceedingly narrow mind; if a Buddha were speaking, hundreds of thousands of different beings would understand in hundreds of thousands of different ways, and if a great Bodhisattva like Manjushri were listening, he would understand the entire meaning of a particular teaching at once. But neither of these is the case. I am not a Buddha and you are not Manjushri, so I can only explain in brief.

I once took a teaching in connection with the Three Kayas and there was a reference to seeing the nature of sickness as the Dharmakaya, the clarity of sickness as the Sambhogakaya, and the form of sickness as the Nirmanakaya. Could you say something about that?

This is basically the same as what I have been talking about. Anything you may consider has the essential quality of the Dharmakaya as the two purities. The Sambhogakaya is the expression of the Dharmakaya as brilliant light, not different from the Dharmakaya. The Sambhogakaya expression as brilliant light has five aspects: the place, time, teacher, retinue, and teaching. These five are mentioned in both Sutra and Tantra traditions, but as the Tantra tradition is very expanded, I did not go into it. The unobstructedness of the brilliant light, inseparable from the essential quality of the Dharmakaya, is the expression of compassion.

6 · Trusting the Lama

Can you explain how one receives blessings to gain realization from devotion to the Lama and the lineage?

Devotion to the Lama is very important. Nowadays there seems to be a lack of trust in the Lama; people do not understand the meaning of devotion, and this lack of trust obstructs the blessings of Dharma. Although many people are involved in Dharma, a lot of important elements are lacking in their attitude. People do not recognize their obligations to sentient beings, and this is one basic fault in Dharma everywhere. Everybody thinks it is up to someone else: Westerners look to Tibetans, Tibetans look to Westerners.

In Tibet, Dharma was for many centuries an important factor in people's lives. Tibetans were conditioned to have faith in the Three Jewels, and whatever they heard about Dharma they instinctively believed. They had a completely blind faith. Tibetans are poor and have fewer material possessions than Westerners, so they concern themselves more with the mind. Whatever they are involved in, whether it is politics, personal relationships, or religion, they think a lot and create many ideas, building up a lot of habits.

In the West there is a lot of skill and learning, but little Dharma. People there are preoccupied with accumulating and manipulating material objects, so they tend to treat Dharma with the same grasping attitude. Westerners are also taught to be active, to work hard, and be speedy. They are concerned with improving the condition of their country, and with maintaining independence and freedom under the law. They create many ideas for the advancement of their country and have many different plans for achieving this end, including various systems of belief and religion. There is a great emphasis on the strength of the country, especially in America, and consequently people need a lot of information. These habits lead them to grasp at ideas and consume them as if they were real. They get used to compiling and accumulating information instead of putting their ideas into practice, and this mental cluttering produces strong habits. This means that when the time comes for them to practice meditation and work with the mind, they find it very difficult. Few Westerners really have pure faith in Dharma. They are attracted to the idea of Dharma, rather than to Dharma practice. Westerners also try to make life easy and remove all the effort from it. They are always saying, "Take it easy." They expect everything to happen at once and very fast, so their minds become unstable as a result of attachment to things that make life easy.

I am not suggesting that Tibetans are especially good or that they have any better habits, but they are poor people and are used to working hard. They work with their minds because there are few distractions in the form of material objects. For this reason there is something of a cultural conflict between Westerners and Tibetans. Westerners are always in a hurry. They find Tibetans extremely slow and think they teach in a ponderous way. The Tibetan custom with Dharma is to be careful, and to Westerners this means painfully sluggish. From the Tibetan point of view Westerners appear unstable; and what Tibetans fear is that Westerners will grab at Dharma as if it were a tube of toothpaste and just throw it away when they cannot get any more out of it. A lot of Tibetans feel that the Western approach will not be of any use either in this life or in the next, because it wastes opportunities and creates no merit. On the other hand, many Westerners hesitate to approach Dharma because of the ponderous pace at which it is taught. They think it must be very difficult to understand, so they do not get involved.

Despite the spread of Dharma in the West, many people there are still power-oriented. They create organizations with power structures and use them for manipulative purposes, so to some extent Dharma is being used in the West as a tool in political power games. Since there are a few good people in Dharma, however, these tendencies may eventually diminish.

Whatever vehicle or level is being practiced, it is essential to trust the law of karma in order to receive blessings. As I explained before, it is false to hold that everything is the creation of some external and omniscient god, or that everything is simply a collection of associated conditions that vanish when their appearances vanish. We should instead recognize that everything arises by the force of the karma created through our own minds. The fruition of good karma is rebirth in the higher realms and the eventual attainment of realization. To set out on the path of devotion and blessings, we must first have an adequate understanding of karma. If we trust the truth of karma, faith will come of itself without our having to do anything about it, and we will automatically receive blessings. Earlier I gave the example of a baby knowing how to suck without having to learn, as an illustration of the way habits are built up. I also tried to show how habits function, with the example of going to sleep at night and dreaming about things related to waking life. These habits are built up through the force of karma created in previous lives, and also lead to the creation of new karma.

It is important to find a Lama or spiritual friend who is in harmony with one's own approach to Dharma. If one is strongly attracted to the practice of ethical precepts and the training of the Vinaya, one should find a teacher who is especially adept at practicing and teaching these. There are certain qualities to look for in a Hinayana spiritual friend. First of all he should understand the precepts. This means he must be familiar with the Pratimoksha and the four sections on the precepts of training, which involves having memorized all the root verses and being able to explain all the precepts. He should also have taken ordination and practiced all the monastic precepts for at least ten years. There are many other qualities of a teacher of the precepts, but they are all contained in these two, as is stated in the Vinaya. Such a teacher will instruct his disciples in all the ways of renouncing the defilements. He must be a total renunciant who has become weary of samsara and can give up the entire universe.

The Mahayana teacher experiences everything as illusion. He has gone beyond the experience of anything as fixed or permanent, and has become skilled in the purification of all the defilements. He must understand the Bodhisattva path and be learned in all the sutras that deal with it. The mind of a teacher of the Mahayana will express compassion without his ever having tried to create it—his compassion must be totally spontaneous. His mind should be open and spacious, and whatever he does for other beings, he must never become exhausted or feel that working for them is in any sense painful or undesirable. He must be able to teach his disciples all the different paths and explain them in a way appropriate to each disciple. There are a great many qualities of a Mahayana teacher but they are all present in the one quality of great compassion.

There are various accounts of the Vajrayana teacher in different tantras, and an exhaustive description would take many days. The tantras mention six, seven, and eight qualities of a Vajrayana teacher, but these can all be described as the tantric master's own experience of the purification of all realms, including the purification of his own experience. Rather than giving up the defilements, the Vajrayana master knows how to use them for the benefit of others. He teaches his disciples how to transform the defilements into wisdom.

Some teachers possess all three sets of qualities. Outwardly they keep the precepts, act like monks, and maintain strict discipline; inwardly they develop the great Bodhisattva attitude of compassion for all beings; and secretly they practice the tantras in their meditation. Others follow the path of the Vinaya and inwardly develop the Mahayana expression of great love and compassion for all sentient beings, but do not approach the tantras. Some seem to be purely tantric and appear not to keep the Hinayana and Mahayana precepts, but close inspection would show that they actually do observe them.

The Hinayana precepts are contained in the Mahayana learning—the learning of bodhichitta—and the Vajrayana precepts embrace both levels. The succeedingly higher levels embrace the precepts of the lower levels, but the lower levels do not contain anything of the higher precepts. In other words, the Hinayana does not contain the Mahayana learning or the Vajrayana precepts, and the Mahayana learning does not contain the Vajrayana precepts.

The Hinayana training teaches renunciation of the defilements. When aversion toward an enemy or desire for a beautiful woman arises in the mind, those defilements are given up by the use of one of the various means taught in the Hinayana. The Mahayana teaches that everything is illusion. The enemy or the beautiful woman and the emotions of aversion or desire are seen as having no reality, and in this way the defilements are pulverized and thus automatically renounced; so giving up the defilements by seeing them as illusory fulfills the Hinayana precepts also. The Vajrayana teaches that all appearances come from our own conceptions, our own thoughts. These seem to be arbitrarily created, but their initial source is in fact the activity of awareness constantly expressing itself. By recognizing all appearances as the activity of awareness, we can learn to use the duality of impure appearances and defilements, and can transform them into wisdom. The teacher must be proficient in at least one of these three levels of practice.

Some Lamas really look like Lamas. They can be identified by their robes and their conduct, and it is obvious that they have the three levels of precepts. Other individuals, although they may not look like Lamas or teachers, may equally have the three levels of precepts through having aroused bodhichitta or through keeping the tantric precepts. Padmasambhava is depicted in thangkas wearing the signs of the three vehicles to symbolize his completion of the three levels of precepts in his own practice. He wears a monk's patched robe symbolizing the Hinayana, the ordinary Tibetan costume symbolizing the Mahayana, and a king's crown symbolizing the Vajrayana. This symbolism is sometimes criticized on the grounds that since Padmasambhava had many consorts, his precepts were not intact, so it is inappropriate for him to wear monk's robes. This shows a misunderstanding of the meaning behind the precepts. The object of Dharma, and therefore of precepts, is realization of the fundamental nature. External purity gives no indication as to whether the fundamental nature is obscured.

This is also illustrated in the life of Saraha. Saraha had been a monk for a long time when he met the daughter of an arrowsmith, and in his relationship with her he attained realization. It was after this that Saraha ordained Nagarjuna and taught him the Vinaya. He said to Nagarjuna, "Before I met the arrowsmith's daughter I was not a pure monk, but after I met her I was a pure monk." This was a reference to his own insight. From an ordinary point of view it would seem that Saraha was a pure monk until he met the arrowsmith's daughter and not so afterward, but the ordinary point of view and that of realization are quite distinct.

I am not trying to suggest that outer precepts are unnecessary. Outer precepts are very useful if they can be kept; we cannot all be like Saraha. We should always keep an open mind and try not to be rigid about these matters. An open mind is very important since it not only forms the basis for the development of bodhichitta and tantric practice, but also prevents unvirtuous action and problematic attitudes. We should feel that if someone takes ordination it is a good thing because it is a way of practicing Dharma. And if it seems that someone is not keeping his precepts very well, we should keep an open mind. We do not know his inner experience, so it is not a matter for us to judge. If we hear that someone who had seemed to be a good monk has left his robes or lost his ordination, we should not start laying down judgments. In the past there have been positive instances of people leaving their robes. One cannot judge another person's experience. If we try to form judgments based only on people's actions, the negative feelings we will arouse toward them will create a lot of unvirtuous action. We will make enemies and create a lot of suffering and problems for ourselves by conflict with others and disturbance in our own minds.

Imagine that one of my friends here was a rigid monk, obsessed with keeping ethical precepts, and that I did not have many precepts but responded to all three vehicles and had studied them a little. If we suddenly learned that another monk we know had married, my friend would be very shocked and angry. He would insult the married monk and so create a lot of unvirtuous action. He would not be able to continue his friendship with the married monk, and his own anger would cause him a lot of suffering. I would feel, however, that possibly the married monk was developing on the path; after he had taken teachings from many Lamas and reached a certain level of insight, marrying was perhaps a sign of his advancement. By keeping an open mind, I would avoid experiencing any suffering myself, and since I would have no negative feelings toward him, we would still be able to be friends. Samsara is suffering, and the real source of samsara is anger. If one is free from anger and suffering, one is free from the source of samsara.

You mentioned that some people lack real faith in the Lama and others suffer from tight minds when they go to see famous Lamas.* Could you say what real faith in the Lama is?

The correct approach to a Lama is to keep an open and relaxed mind, and to develop a pure perception of the Lama, to see him as a very pure being. If we are open about ourselves and keep an open and relaxed mind we will be able to make clear contact with the Lama, free of any defilement from our own mind's ideas. There will be no feeling such as "I am this Lama's disciple" or "This Lama is better than any other Lama." These heavy conceptions will not arise.

If we do not approach the situation in this way, it will be easy to give rise to these defiled attitudes. They are particularly easy to develop; perhaps I am subject to them myself. I noticed these tendencies a good deal in Europe, particularly in those closest to the Lamas, those in the inner circle of disciples of a prominent Lama. People who associate with those Lamas but are not so close to them do not seem to develop those faults to the same degree. So perhaps if you are outer disciples you will remain pure, but if you are in the inner circle, you may already have lost your purity.

In the retinue of a great Lama, we also come across individuals who are able to use these favorable circumstances and develop their meditation by being free of all attachment to the situation. But some people are not always able to use such favorable circumstances so well. This is especially so among scholars. When scholars find themselves in favorable conditions, they often do not know how to work with those conditions and tend to misuse them. They feel improved by their situation and tend to feel proud. They think, "I've mastered all these languages and philosophies, learned all these skills and sciences—I'm really wonderful." When they become proud, if they attain some high position and gain the respect of those around them, they become attached. The misuse of good conditions inevitably creates suffering for them. Some other scholar eventually comes along and displaces them or is thought to be more learned. Or their faculties and skills deteriorate with age, they cannot do so much work, and so they lose the respect they once enjoyed. They feel pain due

*See page 129.

to their loss of respect and position, and they feel jealous because people recognize other scholars as more learned.

Since we started meeting here, I have emphasized the importance of keeping an open mind and not making judgments. I am not a very good example of this myself, since I'm rigid; but I have noticed in the West and other places that despite the spread of Dharma, very few people are open-minded. An open mind enables one to avoid arguments, aggression, and destructive thoughts and activities. Something that happened to me recently illustrates this. I visited a monastery in India where there were a lot of young novices. I knew the abbot was learned in history and philosophy, but during our conversation he said that although he knew very little about these subjects, he thought perhaps he had attained some development in Dzogchen meditation. I had no idea of his meditative abilities and so thought nothing about it. At that point all the novices came into the room to greet me, and began prostrating. There is nothing I like less than people prostrating to me—for one thing, I have no qualities that merit prostration, so I find it embarrassing, and for another, no matter how many people prostrate to me it never does me any good. I immediately told the novices to stop, but the abbot said it did not matter since there were no monks among them. Then I had one of the worst thoughts I could ever have. "If he has developed Dzogchen insight," I thought, "how can he discriminate about who makes prostrations?" It is because of such thoughts that I do not like judgments very much.

If we are always rigid and closed-minded, we will cause a lot of trouble for ourselves and experience many problems in practicing the path. If we keep an open mind all the time, we will avoid causing ourselves any trouble and will develop meditation very easily.

It is possible to overestimate the importance of monkhood. The Sakya family in Tibet is said to be descended from Manjushri and is held in high esteem by Tibetans. Some of its members are not permitted to become monks; they must marry and have children so that the family line can be continued. By contrast, most of the Karmapas were monks, though Khakhyab Dorje, the predecessor of the sixteenth Karmapa, had two wives. This was not a fault; it was probably for the benefit of Dharma.

Since Khakhyab Dorje was initially a monk, his marriage was not widely known of at first, but eventually the word spread and became hot news. There are always jealous and abrasive people in monastic circles—not that those qualities are not found elsewhere—and at this time a Sakya monk and a Karma Kagyu monk happened to meet on a path in the middle of nowhere in particular, and fell into conversation. In keeping with Tibetan custom they exchanged snuff, and the Sakya monk, rather an abrasive character, said, "Well, what's the latest news?" The Kagyu monk replied, "I haven't heard anything interesting at all." The Sakya monk said, "But isn't it true your Lama has lost his ordination and utterly gone to waste? This really is a matter of regret—it's so sad that your Lama's lost his ordination." And the Kagyu monk replied, "Yes, it's very regrettable—he's become just like your Lama."

If one really understands the purpose and importance of the three levels of precept, one's mind will automatically become completely open.

How should we approach a Lama for teaching?

It is important not to be speedy or abrupt. We must examine the teacher and see if he has the appropriate qualities, and we might even do this for as long as twelve years before approaching him for teachings. Even if we come to feel that the teacher knows what he is doing and we approach him for teaching, it may not be appropriate for him to give it immediately. He also has to examine the nature of the disciple. If he were to give teachings immediately, the disciple might just use them like toothpaste. If the Lama examines the disciple on the Hinayana level, he looks to see whether he is attracted to samsara. On the Mahayana level, he looks for compassion and an expansive attitude, and on the Vajrayana level, he looks to see whether the disciple is capable of purifying all his perceptions and concepts.

We would in fact have to be quite learned and skillful to do this; otherwise, we would never discover what faults and qualities a person had, however long we examined him. For this reason it is necessary to know something about Dharma first. It is also important to follow a lineage in order to gain some understanding and appreciation of Dharma. Examining the Lama is a difficult proposition, and if we have no perspective on the three vehicles, our viewpoint will be narrow and we will not really know how to handle the matter.

One might meet an ordained Lama, for example, and be led by his pure conduct to have faith in him, not knowing that he was really a yogi and that his activities were quite different from one's conceptions of them. Having established a connection with him based on erroneous conceptions, one might suddenly realize one's mistake and irrationally lose faith and break the connection with him. This would be the result of not understanding the situation in the first place, so it is vital to gain some understanding and appreciation of the three vehicles.

Not only should the Lama have given up all faults and developed all qualities, the disciple must also perceive this. If there are still faults and flaws in the disciple's own mind, he will see faults and flaws in everything, including the Lama.

If one does not know how to purify one's experience, meeting or following even a hundred Lamas will be of no benefit because one will continue to see impurity. Someone looking for a teacher might begin by following a Lama of great purity. Eventually he might be troubled by the thought "This Lama may be pure but he is not much of a scholar; there is not much to be learned from him." So he would leave that Lama to follow someone more learned. After spending some time with the scholar, he might come to feel that his new teacher, while certainly very learned, was proud of his learning, so he would try to find someone more humble. He might then find some little-known Lama who seemed free of pride. But at some moment when he happened to be experiencing some bad karma, he might feel, "This Lama is humble but he is also rather stingy." And having seen a fault, he would go on to someone else. He might meet an unordained yogi and decide immediately, "This person has far too many desires to be a teacher." Then he might follow a monk again, but when more bad karma ripened, he might come to feel, "This monk is superficially pure, but in the depths of his heart he is debauched." And having seen yet another fault, he would leave that teacher, too.

In this way one would cause oneself a lot of confusion and suffering; so what one has to do is give up all standards, all ideas of ever examining or judging anything, and be completely open. In the sutras and tantras there are exhaustive instructions for examining a teacher, but applying them in detail is very hard. In brief, a Lama must have given up ordinary faults and have developed his potential.

A further account of the Lama's qualities is the general description of the levels of teaching in terms of the five paths. If a disciple is on the path of the accumulation of merit and wisdom, his Lama should at least be on the path of connection. If the disciple has reached the path of connection, his Lama should at least have reached the path of seeing. If the disciple is on the path of seeing, the Lama should at least have reached the path of meditation; and if the disciple is on the path of meditation, the Lama should have reached the path of no more learning. In other words, the Lama should be at least one stage higher than his disciple.

Having made the choice to approach a particular Lama, one must request the teachings one aspires to, and if one's karma is right at that particular moment, the Lama will give the appropriate teaching. But if not, one may experience that the Lama puts problems in one's way. He may cause difficulties by being hard; he may delay for a long time or only a little. So it is important to be patient and not expect to get what one wants immediately. These difficulties are intended to prepare the disciple and make him a suitable vessel to receive the teachings. But a few Lamas give their disciples a lot of trouble for no reason whatsoever. It is impossible to decide what a Lama's motives are.

Once we have set out to follow a particular Lama and received his instructions, we must never allow doubts to interfere with the relationship. We must give up all doubts and have a direct attitude toward him. It does not matter whether the Lama is impure or pure, whether his habits are bad or good, or whether his appearance is unpleasant or pleasant. It does not matter if his lifestyle seems contrary to the Dharma—for instance, if he hunts, or if his lifestyle is generally despised, such as prostitution. We must never allow doubts to interfere with our relationship with the Lama once we have decided to follow him and take his instructions. Doubt is the greatest enemy and the biggest obstacle to the practice of tantra.

Marpa the Translator caused Milarepa a lot of trouble. This had nothing to do with any selfish motivation on Marpa's part, but was for the purpose of training Milarepa. Tilopa also gave his disciple Naropa a lot of trouble. Naropa was a learned pandita who had been a prominent figure at Vikramashila monastic university for some time when he decided to seek a teaching that would enable him to attain realization in one lifetime.

He received a prophecy in a dream that the great siddha Tilopa was to be his Lama, so he set out to look for him. Tilopa was not famous at that time, so it was extremely difficult for Naropa to find him. Wherever he went, he would ask if anyone knew where the great siddha Tilopa was, but no one had ever heard of such a person. Naropa went on like this until someone said, "I've never heard of the great siddha Tilopa, but that fellow over there is the old beggar Tilopa."

Tilopa was sitting eating fish. He would eat one and snap his fingers, then eat another and snap his fingers, and Naropa's first thought on seeing him was, "What a terrible fellow, eating all those fish." Then he remembered that this was the man prophesied as his Lama and decided to make a prayer of supplication. "Great Tilopa," he said, "I pray that you will take me as your disciple and look on me with compassion."

"I'm just an old beggar," Tilopa replied. "I don't have any compassion to look on anyone with." But he took Naropa with him anyway. Naropa soon saw that Tilopa had neither house nor occupation; he was constantly on the move, wandering from place to place, and the only thing he ever did was play children's games.

Tilopa made life very hard for Naropa. On one occasion when they were both very hungry, Tilopa sent him into the forest to beg for food. Naropa approached some people who were having lunch and was given a large bowl of soup, which he offered to Tilopa. Tilopa liked the soup, and Naropa was so glad to have been able to please his Lama that he went back into the forest to get some more. The people he had begged from seemed to have gone, but the soup was still there. Naropa was just helping himself to it when one of them returned, caught him red-handed, and beat him up. Another time, Tilopa promised to give Naropa teachings if he jumped from the top of a very high stupa. Naropa obediently followed his Lama's instructions and was badly injured, but received no teachings.

Once Tilopa said, "A marriage procession will pass along this road in a few minutes. When it comes by, I want you to scatter flowers of greeting, chant some auspicious verses, and place a garland around the bride's neck. Then grab her by the breasts." The procession came by just as Tilopa had said it would, and Naropa did what Tilopa had told him—and got another beating.

One day Naropa was carrying a bucket of water along a path when Tilopa suddenly hit him over the head with a shoe and said, "Look at your own mind. Recognize your own fundamental nature—I can't tell you anything." Naropa passed out from the force of the blow, and when he recovered, Tilopa's wisdom had arisen in him and he recognized the nature of his own mind. This happened because he had great faith in his Lama, and because Tilopa was a great siddha who had many blessings.

There are many different ways of serving the Lama, and in various texts we find accounts of the appropriate way of approaching him, prostrating to him, addressing him, and listening to his teachings. However, people seldom have sufficient faith in the Lama nowadays, and if they were to serve him in the traditional manner and suffer hardships at his hands, they would probably begin to have doubts and suspect him of exploiting them for his own selfish ends. It is for this reason that the preliminary practices are usually given. They are not necessary in themselves, but are another way of approaching the Lama and developing insight.

Motivation is of the utmost importance in approaching Dharma. In the Hinayana, one adopts an attitude of renunciation, while the Mahayana demands the expansive attitude of aspiring to liberate all beings from suffering. When listening to the teachings, one should place the Lama on a throne and imagine him as Buddha Shakyamuni, the original teacher of Dharma, and his disciples as Arhats and Shravakas if one is following the Hinayana, or as Bodhisattvas if one is following the Mahayana.

It is important to give up certain faults in listening to the teachings, such as what are called the three faults of a pot. An inverted pot will never contain anything no matter how much one tries to pour into it: if one does not concentrate on the teachings, one will never learn anything no matter how much one hears. A pot with a hole in the bottom will not retain anything for long: if the teachings are not kept in mind, they will seep away and one will be left with nothing. If a pot has a poison in it, anything poured into it will be corrupted: if one listens to the teachings with defiled motivation, such as seeking fame or respect, whatever one hears will become defiled. One should listen to the teachings with the intention to attain realization and free all beings from suffering.

Another series of faults in listening to the teachings is known as the six stains. These are pride, lack of faith, lack of application, outer distraction, keeping the mind so locked in that one hears nothing, and a depressed attitude. The five wrong modes of perception also concern defiled attitudes toward the Lama and the teachings. These are seeing oneself as a hunter, the Lama as a musk deer, and the teachings as musk; pursuing the teachings the way a hunter hunts a deer; and considering the results of the teachings as aggrandizing to oneself. In approaching Dharma we should develop the idea of ourselves as patients, the Lama as a doctor, the teachings as medicine, and our practice as a course of treatment. There are a great many lists and categories in Tibetan tradition concerning incorrect and correct attitudes toward the Lama and the teachings, but since you are not Tibetans it would probably just bore you if I went into them all. Instead I would like to look at the question of relationship with a Lama from a different angle.

First we must determine whether the Lama is an Indian, a Tibetan, or a Westerner; and if he is a Westerner, we must determine whether he is English, French, American, or from somewhere else in the West. If he is a Tibetan, we have to determine whether he is from Eastern Tibet, Western Tibet, or Central Tibet. It is commonly maintained by Eastern Tibetans that the vast majority of great Lamas have come from Eastern Tibet [Kham]. However, although Khampas are very proud of this, it is not particularly accurate: two of the greatest Lamas in history, Longchen Rabjam and Jigme Lingpa, came from Central Tibet, and Sakya Pandita came from Western Tibet. A large number of great Lamas of the Nyingma, Sakya, and Kagyu lineages were indeed natives of Eastern Tibet, but there is no truth in upholding any one place as the source of all great Lamas. China and the Soviet Union are two nations that not only seem to have few great Lamas, but also maintain that they do not need them.

Ancient Tibet and India no longer exist. We are in a new situation now, so perhaps we should have some new ideas on this question of approaching a Lama. First it is important to examine the Lama to see what he is doing. Many Lamas have completely changed their style since they left Tibet. It is a mistake to feel that there is anything wrong with this; the mistake would be trying to perpetuate the style they had in Tibet. When the place changes, the individual changes; and if the Bodhisattva did not modify his expression in a new place, he could not work appropriately for the beings in that place. As a monk, my friend here has no desire to dance. If he wanted to offer flowers to his altar in a place where Dharma had been spread, he probably would not have any difficulty. He could go up to some person who had faith in Dharma—some local woman digging in her garden, perhaps—and ask for some flowers. If she had faith in Dharma, she would give them to him. But if he were suddenly to find himself in a country where people were hostile to Dharma and he wanted to offer flowers to his altar, he might approach some woman working in the garden and ask for some flowers, and she might say, "If you want some flowers, you'll have to dance with me first." Like it or not, he would have to dance with her in order to get the flowers for his altar. As this example shows, one should not take a judgmental attitude toward someone who changes his lifestyle or mode of expression from one place to another.

Places change people, and an activity appropriate to one place is not necessarily appropriate to another. We should not impose arbitrary standards on Dharma by consulting books to see how things were done in ancient Tibet and then slavishly apply those standards. We should feel out the real situation, see what is appropriate to it, and act accordingly. This may appear tricky, but it is not really so at all; it is actually very simple. The question of how to make contact with a Lama has arisen, so we have to deal with that. We should examine the Lama to find out if he is a monk or not and what kind of work or activities he likes. This is best done directly with the Lama himself, but if that is not possible we should make contact with the people closest to him. We should try to discover what kind of character he has, whether he resembles the general Eastern Tibetan type (direct, blunt, and straightforward) or the Central Tibetan type (formal and reserved). Central Tibetans resemble English and French people in this respect: a Central Tibetan Lama or an English or French Lama would tend to be serious and formal, not very direct. There is no need to get worked up over this question. We just gradually work into a style somewhat similar to the Lama's in order to relate to him. If he is very direct and straightforward and says whatever is on his mind, we should adopt a similar approach by responding to him with whatever is on our own mind.

Some teachers may have the style of their own locality and act in accordance with the customs they have become used to, but this is not always the case. Some people, especially siddhas, discard their native customs completely, and in such a case we learn nothing by finding out their local customs since they themselves do not follow any of them. The real standard to adopt is to act in a way that pleases the Lama, ascertaining how he wants us to act and behaving accordingly. If our actions do not inspire the teacher's confidence, it will be impossible for us to absorb and develop his wisdom and qualities.

Sometimes there are obnoxious people around a Lama who can cause a lot of trouble and obstacles. We must learn to be patient with this. If we disagree with the Lama's wife or his attendant, for example, we should never talk about it to others—we should just be patient and let it pass. This attitude should be applied to the whole environment surrounding the Lama.

If you have trouble making contact with the Lama or problems with people around him, begin by making your presence felt. At the very least, go into his room and stand in a place where he can see you. Even if you never say anything, if you keep showing up and if the Lama is really pure, he will eventually say, "What are you doing here? You must want something to keep coming back all the time." When you get this opportunity, you should say what is on your mind. If the Lama is a bad person, he will establish the position beyond all doubt at this point and you will know that you never have to return.

But it is not really possible to be as absolute as that. Even if both the Lama and the disciple are pure, if the karma is not good, the circumstances may work out badly and it may be difficult to make contact. We should not feel negative toward the Lama in a case like this, but should recognize that such difficulties are due to bad karma. We should pray again and again that we will be able to make good contact with our Lama. When actually relating to the Lama, we may occasionally experience what would seem to be strange things. It may appear that the Lama is making a lot of judgments and being very opinionated, or that he is making mistakes. If this happens, think about whether you are not mistaken yourself. If he seems to be making judgments, try to see that appearance as just your own judgment and keep an open mind. Our own bad karma may make it seem as though the Lama is doing unusual things that are at odds with our expectations.

Sometimes our circumstances are favorable. We are happy, we have money in our pockets, it is easy to approach the Lama and have good contact with him, and easy to meditate and develop insight. But the worst enemy of practice is an inability to come down to earth at a time when things are going well. We all have some development and some understanding of Dharma; but if we allow ourselves to get carried away when circumstances are good, we will never be able to come down to earth or make contact with the Lama and do the practice when it is easiest and when things can be done the best. This applies equally to everybody, ordained or not, Tibetan or Western. Many Westerners want to learn something about Dharma. They become obsessed by this and feel that they should go to see some great Lama, and this is certainly a very good idea. But many of these prominent Lamas are power symbols in our minds, and so people sometimes get way up in the air about them. These people create unfavorable circumstances for themselves. I never pretend to be a Lama, and when I went to Europe I just approached people as a friend and they approached me in the same way. People would come around and talk, much as we are doing now, and I would just try to talk about Dharma as best I could. In these circumstances people would come down to earth and be very simple, so they would create a much better atmosphere, much better perhaps than in the company of a great Lama. This is not to say that I am jealous of great Lamas, of course, but it seemed that people could find out about Dharma much better in an informal atmosphere where their own attitudes created fewer obstacles.

Whatever else we do, in approaching Dharma we must receive the teachings from the Lama and practice them just as he indicates. It is not enough just to imitate the external features of practice. This only leads to a scattered mind and an inability to achieve any integrated development on the path. This results in a surly and aggressive character.

Whether or not the Lama is a monk and no matter what his style, if we always work at developing his qualities in ourselves, our mind will naturally become open and at ease. Our own qualities will always increase and our motivation will become increasingly purer. But if we are unable to adopt a balanced attitude, going to see great Lamas is of no benefit and may even make things worse. Even if the teacher is completely pure, if the student does not know how to take advantage of the opportunity of contact with him, he may only succeed in fouling it up. For example, nowadays there are many philosophically inclined people who go to a scholarly Lama and learn many things about philosophy. They may study for a long time, but in the end it may not benefit them at all. In fact, it often harms them, because they may become proud of their knowledge and tend to feel that people who study with other Lamas are really nowhere, the other Lamas are not learned, they do not know much at all, and what they do know they have not gotten straight. When they read a Dharma book, people like this will say it is full of mistakes, and when they go to see a Lama, they will think he does not know anything. They formulate negative attitudes toward everything, and this is the root of paranoia.

The long and the short of relating to the Lama is trying to please him. If the Lama likes monks, become a monk. If he likes building monasteries, build him a monastery. If he likes sex, sleep with him—whatever he likes, try to please him.

The body is not a stable condition. One day we are going to lose it, so if we do not know how to relate to the teacher now in order to create some benefit, we will be creating a lot of suffering for ourselves.

We're taught to say, "I take refuge in the Buddha as the doctor, I take refuge in the Dharma as the medicine, I take refuge in the Sangha as the nurse." So do you think it's useful if I go back to the West wearing my nun's robes, so that I'm recognizable as a sort of nurse? Do you think I can help more people that way?

It is a very great blessing to wear the robes of ordination. Buddha Shakyamuni said that whoever wears these robes is a good person merely by wearing them. Simply wearing these robes is said to purify many obscurations, such as those that arise due to handling objects and receiving gifts. Robes are a symbol of the Sangha, one of the Three Jewels, and it is useful for people that there should be monks and nuns in the West wearing robes. But many people today have the idea that the word *Sangha* only means monks and nuns, so most of the people here in this room would not be considered Sangha because they are not ordained. This is true from a Hinayana point of view, since in the Hinayana, *Sangha* means monks and nuns. But from the Mahayana point of view this is not exactly the case. The Tibetan word for Sangha means "all those who have a concentrated virtuous intention." This specifically refers to keeping precepts: in the

Hinayana keeping the Hinayana precepts, and in the Mahayana observing the bodhichitta precepts of acting for all sentient beings. The Vajrayana Sangha are those who keep the tantric precepts, so not only monks and nuns but all those who keep the precepts of Dharma in any of the vehicles are also members of the Sangha. In the Mahayana we also speak of the Arya Sangha, or the sublime followers of virtue. The word *arya,* or "sublime," refers to the expansive attitude of the Mahayana. Those who take the Vajrayana precepts must also have a certain number of Hinayana and Mahayana precepts, at least the refuge and bodhichitta precepts. Those who take the Vajrayana precepts and keep them are referred to in Tibetan as "members of the family of the tantric Sangha." So keep an open mind about the idea of Sangha. There are different levels of the Hinayana, Mahayana, and Vajrayana Sangha, and the idea of Sangha varies from one level to another. Being a monk or nun is no obstacle to practicing either the Mahayana or the Vajrayana. It is even said occasionally that being a monk or nun can be useful in approaching the tantras.

7 · Refuge

There are three ways to enter the Vajrayana: from the beginning, along the path, and from the fruition. Entering from the fruition means approaching the path stage by stage, passing through the Hinayana and the Mahayana and then gradually through the tantras—Kriya, Charya or Upa, Yoga, Maha, Anu, and Ati. In this approach, one has to attain the fruit of each stage before practicing the next. Entering along the path means developing some of the qualities of the path without necessarily developing the fruition fully. Entering from the beginning is known as King Indrabodhi's approach. King Indrabodhi came to Dharma with no apparent grounding in either the sutras or the outer tantras, and practiced the inner tantras from the very beginning. However, we cannot be absolutely certain that King Indrabodhi had never practiced the lower levels of the path and attained their realization, since he might have done so in previous lives.

King Indrabodhi was walking on the roof of his palace one day when he saw a number of people flying through the air. This was rather surprising to him, so he asked Chandrabhadra, one of his ministers, who these people were. Chandrabhadra replied that they were disciples of Buddha Shakyamuni, a fully enlightened Buddha whose disciples had attained realization and developed miraculous and supernormal powers. This caused Indrabodhi to have a lot of faith in Buddha Shakyamuni. If the disciples had attained such powers, he thought, the teacher himself must have very great qualities.

We should not think that these ancient accounts of people flying through the air without the aid of hang gliders are just tall tales and have no objective truth; an individual who has developed insight and transcended conceptual bonds such as those relating to the body will have unlimited abilities. Since we are subject to the obscurations of ignorance and are experiencing the physical body, the fruition of the karma we have created on the path, we are not able to fly, but this does not mean that people who have different faculties and abilities cannot do so. In an earlier discussion we saw that the body, and all phenomenal appearance, is an expression of the mind and that there is no more or less reality in dreams than in the waking state. Sometimes we dream of flying, and since the world is as illusory as a dream, it might also be possible to fly in the waking state.

King Indrabodhi said to Chandrabhadra that Buddha Shakyamuni must be very great and powerful, and that he would very much like to meet him, but even a king could hardly expect such a great and powerful man to come especially to visit him. Indrabodhi's palace was a long way from the territory of the Shakya clan, and it would be very difficult for Buddha Shakyamuni to cover such a great distance, as there were no cars or trains in those days. Chandrabhadra replied that this did not matter. The Buddha's wisdom had no particular location, he said, and one could certainly meet him by praying one-pointedly. Indrabodhi did many prostrations in the direction of Buddha Shakyamuni's abode, making strong prayers to him to come to the palace, and by the powers of miraculous manifestation, Buddha Shakyamuni and a large number of disciples flew through the air and appeared at the palace.

Indrabodhi gave a great feast for Buddha Shakyamuni and all the disciples, and requested a teaching that would enable him to attain the full realization of Buddhahood. Buddha Shakyamuni said that Indrabodhi would first have to give up everything and take ordination as a monk. Indrabodhi replied that he was not able to do this. He wanted a teaching by which he would be able to attain realization without having to give up any of his wives, his friends, his ministers, his palace, his kingdom, or his possessions. All the disciples around Buddha Shakyamuni, who were really manifestations of Bodhisattvas, vanished into the air, and a supernatural sound was heard in the sky. Buddha Shakyamuni then transformed himself into the Guhyasamaja mandala and began teaching Indrabodhi the Guhyasamaja practice, one of the inner tantras. He initiated the king and all his retinue into the Guhyasamaja mandala and introduced the true nature during the initiation. Most of us are not like King Indrabodhi. I do not have the insight to see who is like him, but I certainly am not. Such a person must have a very great mind completely free of all doubt.

One must assess one's individual approach to the Dharma. One might be attracted to the Sutra tradition, but this is no reason to disparage those who try to approach Dharma directly through the tantras. If one is attracted to the Sutra tradition, one must begin by taking refuge precepts, upasaka precepts, or the precepts of a novice or a monk. The refuge of the sutras is automatically contained in the tantric refuge, although the reverse is not the case. To set out on the tantric path it is necessary to start with the preliminary practices, but any Dharma practice begins with taking refuge, whether in the Hinayana, the Mahayana, or the Vajrayana. Some people feel that it is necessary to take refuge, even though they have received a tantric initiation. But if they really understood the nature of Dharma, or even if they were just somewhat learned, they would know that the structure of an initiation always includes taking refuge.

In the Hinayana refuge, the teacher is seen as the one who shows the way to Arhatship, the teachings as the path to realization, and the disciples as friends on the path, and in this way one takes refuge in the Three Jewels. In the Mahayana the teacher is seen as Buddha, and his nature is inherently the Three or the Four Kayas,* or aspects of realization. Dharma is seen as the path to realization of full Buddhahood, and the Sangha as the Arya Sangha or assembly of Bodhisattvas. Both the Hinayana and Mahayana refuges are taken as objective: Buddha as the teacher, Dharma as the path, and Sangha as the friends on the path are considered to have an independent, external existence.

One should not take refuge just for a short period, but until attaining realization—until attaining Arhatship in Hinayana terms, and until realizing one's own nature as the Three Kayas and attaining full Buddhahood in Mahayana terms. It is generally said in the Mahayana that it is necessary to take refuge for three infinite eons to create the accumulation of merit, and three infinite eons to purify obscurations. This is by no means absolute, however. Some people may take a very long time to attain realization,

*The Four Kayas include the Svabhavikakaya along with the Three Kayas.

and others may attain it very quickly if their karma is good. There is no reason to despair over the great length of time it may take.

In the tantras the three refuges are contained in the Lama, Yidam, and Khandro. The Lama is the enlightened nature of the three, four, or five aspects of realization, and the Yidam and Dakini are expressions or modes of appearance of the Lama and not in any sense different from him. The special quality of the Lama is to confer blessings, the Yidam is taught as an expression of realization, and the Dakini is taught for the purpose of dispelling obstacles and performing enlightened activities. There are many methods of practicing the various Lamas, Yidams, and Dakinis. Although these are taught for slightly different purposes and express slightly different aspects and attributes of deities, their essence is the same. There are many different Lama practices, such as Guru Rinpoche, many Yidam practices, such as Phurba and Chechog,* and many Dakini practices, such as Naljorma and Tröma. They are all taught out of the same essential quality, and it makes little difference which class of deity one practices.

The Tibetan word *lama*† is composed of the two syllables *la* and *ma*. *La* means "the support or basis of the life force," and this points to the extreme importance of the Lama: without basic life force there can be no life. *Ma* means "mother." This refers to the kindness and compassion of a mother in looking after her children, although kindness and compassion in this case are not limited to a few children. The Lama's compassion reaches all sentient beings. By following a Lama, we can develop all the qualities of the path, all the qualities of realization, but without a Lama this is impossible. Similarly, the mundane skills of compassionate action can only be developed in relationship with the Lama. The Tibetan word *yidam*‡ means "consciously taking and holding a vow." When practicing on the path, we must promise never to abandon the Yidam deity until enlightenment is reached, hence the name Yidam. The Tibetan word for Dakini is *khandro*;§ *kha* means "space" and refers to the Dharmadhatu, the fundamental inherent space of the basic nature, and *dro* means "to

---

*che mchog; sometimes phoneticized as *chemchog*.

†bla ma.

‡yi dam.

§mkha' 'gro.

act or move with awareness," so *khandro* means "the movement of the awareness of wisdom in the basic space of Dharmadhatu."

In the practice of the development and completion stages of Mahayoga and Anuyoga, one takes refuge until all phenomena are perceived as the deities of the mandala. Although in our ordinary condition of grasping at duality we do not experience the mandala of the deities, the fundamental enlightened nature is not separate from us; it is still inherent in us. Imagining a field of refuge such as the Three Jewels and taking refuge in it at this level is known as the basic refuge, and practicing teachings based on this refuge is called the refuge of the path. In Mahayana practice, one develops the accumulations of merit and wisdom, and in the Vajrayana, one develops the qualities of insight. In this way, one develops the inherent qualities of the field of refuge,* initially conceived of as external, and in their development and expression, the field of refuge changes from an external object to which one aspires and becomes something internal recognized in one's mind. This refuge in the nature of one's own mind as the Three Jewels is called the refuge of fruition. But it is not possible to take this refuge without the experience of the mind's inherent qualities as the enlightened nature and as long as an external refuge is still needed as a symbol of enlightenment. Since the law of karma is absolutely unerring, if one prays to the outer refuge and does the practices of the path continuously and with great faith, the inner qualities of the field of refuge will inevitably be developed. One will recognize that there is no dual structure of outer realm and inner mind, or realized nature and individual. One will recognize all the qualities of Buddhahood as inherent in mind, and will be able to take refuge in the fundamental nature of mind as the nature of the Three Jewels.

But at the moment it is only possible for us to take this refuge in the sense of hearing about it, not in the sense of appreciating its meaning. If we connect with a good Lama who can introduce the fundamental nature, and if we meditate on his teachings, even without practicing much conceptual virtuous action we will be taking the ultimate or absolute refuge. This is not something we can understand just by hearing about it. It can only be shown.

*tshogs zhing.

Refuge in the Three Jewels is complete in meditation on the true nature of mind. The true nature itself is inherently free of ignorance, and the meaning of Buddhahood is that all ignorance is completely purified and all qualities of enlightenment are fully expanded. Since there is no ignorance in this condition, this meditation is a refuge in the Buddha. Dharma is taught to enable sentient beings to attain realization. It is said that there are eighty-four thousand volumes of Dharma scriptures, divided into Vinaya, Sutra, and Abhidharma. Sometimes the tantra collection is also included. All these teachings have been given so that sentient beings can recognize the fundamental nature of their own minds. In recognizing that fundamental nature, one takes refuge in Dharma. Dharma consists of dharmas of teachings and dharmas of realization. A dharma of teaching is an instruction, such as to refrain from killing, whereas the feeling in one's mind that one is not going to kill but strive to protect life is a dharma of realization. If one maintains meditation on fundamental awareness, all the dharmas of teaching and realization are present. If awareness remains unobscured in meditation, this is actual Dharma. As we saw in the discussion on the Hinayana, Mahayana, and Vajrayana Sangha, each tradition has its own exposition on the meaning of Sangha. As applied to meditation, however, the meaning of this word is quite different. The Tibetan word for Sangha is *gendun*.* *Ge* means "virtue": when one meditates on fundamental awareness, there is neither virtue nor lack of virtue because this recognition is beyond either state. The recognition of this is *dun*, which literally means "mental force," so recognizing fundamental awareness is Sangha, and so in meditation one takes refuge in the Sangha. Therefore, meditating on fundamental awareness embraces both the Mahayana refuge in the Three Jewels and the Vajrayana refuge in the Three Roots [Lama, Yidam, and Khandro].

The Mahayana refuge of the Three Jewels and the Vajrayana refuge of the Three Roots are also present in the Three Kayas. The fundamental nature has no substantiality. It has no essence of its own, no shape or color, and not any ordinary attribute. Dharmakaya is not merely empty; it expresses itself as brilliant light, and this brilliant light nature is Sambhogakaya. Sambhogakaya is not other than Dharmakaya, but simply a

*dge 'dun.

way of considering Dharmakaya, an aspect of it. Essential emptiness and natural brilliance are of themselves evenly pervasive and unobstructed. This is Nirmanakaya. Thus, these three aspects of the enlightened nature are naturally complete in awareness.

In some texts it is said that the Three Jewels are present in the nature of one's own mind. This is a very general statement and not strictly accurate; the Three Kayas are in fact present in fundamental awareness. In the recognition of fundamental awareness there is inherently no obscuration or defilement, so the Three Kayas are expressed. But the mind is itself an erroneous concept, so it is not absolutely correct to refer to the Three Kayas as inherent in the mind.

Today and on other occasions I have spoken a little about the nature of mind and given some special teachings about it. These may seem to be simple and perhaps very beautiful. But they are not generally given; I have mentioned them because I hope they will be useful to you in developing in your meditation. Normally the Hinayana, Mahayana, and Vajrayana refuges are taught, but the refuge as the nature of awareness is kept more secret. This is not just stinginess or secrecy for its own sake, but is intended to prevent people from getting confused. People might feel that if the fundamental refuge is the basic nature, there is no need for an external refuge, and they would cease to take refuge in the Lama and the Three Jewels. They would think there was no need for a teacher and no need for a lineage. They would refer only to their own minds, and in this way they would never understand the basic nature of their own minds. In the West many people do follow a teacher, but sometimes they have doubts about the need to do so and in general they find it very difficult. If it were widely thought that the only refuge was the nature of the mind, people might cease to follow a teacher altogether. It is for this reason that the teachings on the fundamental nature as the only refuge are generally kept secret.

Whatever teachings one takes, it is very important to meditate on them. This will enable one to develop great qualities in Dharma. Without meditation, no matter how much teaching one hears, no matter how much teaching one writes down, no matter how much teaching one records on tape, one will never be able to develop the qualities of Dharma. By meditating on the teachings, one can develop great qualities since the essential meditation on the fundamental nature has no finite bounds of any kind. If one understands the fundamental nature, one can explain Dharma in infinite numbers of ways.

8 · Actual Recognition

People practice Dharma in different ways according to their personal aspirations and inclinations. Some are drawn to ethical precepts, while others cannot stand them and prefer a completely open approach to Dharma. If we want to understand different kinds of people in order to help them, a basic understanding of Dharma is needed. Otherwise, we might fall into the error of creating absolute standards. Such a prescriptive attitude would make us cut people off from the teachings through failing to understand how to approach them in their own context. Without basic insight, we might exclude those who do not feel inclined to monastic ordination, we might exclude monks from the Vajrayana, or we might exclude women from Dharma altogether.

The basic insight of Dharma comes from an understanding of the fundamental nature of mind. Ignorance of how to use Dharma properly just turns it into a disorganized hodgepodge, a source of self-oppression and busyness. It just causes a lot of trouble: you cannot eat, you cannot sleep, you cannot do this, you cannot do that, you cannot make love, you cannot get drunk. An inability to implement Dharma skillfully makes it completely useless, but when properly applied, Dharma can be a source of ultimate happiness.

There used to be many monks in Tibet, some of whom were very open-minded in their outlook. They kept their precepts and functioned entirely as monks, but they did not criticize people or judge their standards. They were equally willing to teach men or women, monks or nuns, or laypeople, whether the students seemed to others to be appropriate vessels for the teachings or not. They did not make any judgments about the matter because they understood the essential quality of the precepts. Thoughts of violating their precepts—such as the impulse to get drunk or to sleep with a woman—just did not occur to them, so they did not feel it necessary to impose ideas about them on anyone else. But there was another type of monk who adopted monastic precepts rather like objects and tried to avoid all the situations that are prohibited in the sutras. For example, it is said that a monk should not talk with a woman or walk along a road within a certain distance of a woman. These monks would try to avoid each and every one of these situations literally and would become so tense that they would actually be afraid. If a woman came within a foot of them, they would jump in fear.

It is most important to keep a completely open mind about everything. Then all the principles of Dharma will be your friends. If you approach Dharma with a rigid attitude, all its principles will become your enemies. In the Kagyu tradition it is said that if Dharma is practiced as it should be practiced, it can only lead to liberation; but if it is practiced against its own principles, it will lead back into the lower realms.

Would it be correct to say that anybody doing the preliminary practices has already entered the Vajrayana path?

I cannot decide if you are entering the Vajrayana. None of you are my disciples, and I do not think of myself as anybody's teacher. I have come here as a friend just to talk and have no reason to examine anybody, and I would not like to undertake such a busy venture. When I said that one must start with the preliminary practices in the Vajrayana, I was speaking in connection with the levels of practice in harmony with the way the teaching is usually given. It is certainly true that in order to approach the Vajrayana one must start with preliminary practice, but it does not follow that someone performing the preliminary practices should necessarily be approaching the Vajrayana. This can only be appreciated in association with one's Lama.

I do not like examining people and things. I've grown weary of it. In all cultures, people examine everything they do. There are ways of examining men and examining women, ways of examining places, gems, and all kinds of things to discover their characteristics. I have actually learned a good deal about this, but I find that as soon as one tries to examine things, one sees something wrong in them. One imagines flaws in the external world and in oneself, and this disturbs the purity of things, so I do not like doing it. If one leaves things alone without ever examining them, they remain just as they are.

If I did examine things, then of course I could see what they are like. If I examined someone I know quite well, I could tell immediately from some habit he had, such as nervously drumming his fingers, that he was constantly involved in speedy thoughts and that this speediness made him careless. He might even run the risk of falling off cliffs if he went about without looking where he was going. In fact, I do have a friend like that. I spoke to him about his speediness the other day, but I was not worried about his reaction because we have known each other for some time. I knew he would listen to me without getting angry. In a case like that there might be some purpose to examining, but otherwise the idea of examining anything usually leads to conflict rather than to benefiting people. I would much rather just leave things as they are.

It can be useful to apply examination for purposes of Dharma, but otherwise it is usually counterproductive. If I were sitting and talking with one of my friends and another person came and joined us, we might create an inimical situation by adopting an examining attitude toward him. We might decide for some reason that he was very proud, and feel the impulse to communicate this. We might suddenly say to each other, "This guy is really weird. He is so arrogant." This would offend him, and we would have created a hostile situation for no reason at all. The third person was not coming in with inimical intentions; he was just coming along to visit us. Even if we did not communicate our perception of a flaw, we would still have created an erroneous concept. And even if we never communicated or used it, that erroneous concept would reinforce the ignorance principle in our minds. All this would have started from the erroneous premise of examination. It would be much better if we just took a completely open attitude, without any judgments, examinations, or discursive ideas whatever. People come and people go; it does not disturb anything at all.

If one wishes to examine anything, a very subtle approach is needed. Few people are capable of this. Most people apply examination only in a very gross sense. The most difficult obstacles to overcome in meditation are subtle conceptions.

Gross conceptions are easy to recognize because they are so gross, and consequently they do not create such an obstacle. Politicians, especially very high-level politicians, often look like siddhas, realized men. They have a very austere demeanor and do not speak much. They consider everything carefully; and what they do say, they say precisely. They maintain an inscrutable and enigmatic pose, and one can never divine their feelings. They can seem peaceful and happy no matter how bad the circumstances, and can be extremely angry about something but still appear unruffled. By contrast, a good number of siddhas have no cares for anything in the world, yet are quite openly obstreperous.

There are also Dharma politicians, and some of them may also look as if they have a high level of realization. They speak softly, conduct themselves well, and are very careful and considerate. They always look as if they are happy. In the case of both ordinary politicians and Dharma politicians, their outer appearance does not correspond at all to their real state of mind. There are many subtle and deep flaws in their minds, which do not receive any outward expression. People who are politically active have to be careful not to insult or denigrate others openly. Nevertheless, they often do so unintentionally. When a politician is praising somebody, one can often see that his praise is actually an insult. This occurs even in Dharma politics. Members of one sect will never disparage another sect, but the tone of their praise will show what they are really thinking. In the same way, gross conceptions are very easy to apprehend in meditation and one can understand them right away, but subtle conceptions are much more difficult to apprehend.

It is these subtle conceptions that can deceive and confuse one. A beginner can often sit in meditation for a couple of hours at a time, and he may find it quite easy to avoid confusion from gross conceptions, but even if he has a little experience with the nature of the mind, he still may be unable to allow it to rest in the fundamental nature. This is because he does not recognize subtle conceptions as they arise, so they continue to cause confusion. Water never stays completely still; it moves or flows in patterns. But if it is flowing in a field where there is a lot of foliage and undergrowth, these will conceal its movement. Subtle conceptions, the small movements in the mind, are likewise concealed, so one fails to recognize them. If these subtle conceptions are not recognized, one cannot liberate them. If one is only a beginner in meditation, one should not push oneself too hard. Take a slow and easy approach with an open and relaxed mind, and do not try to force recognition of subtle conceptions.

How do you liberate conceptions once you have recognized them?

The very act of recognition frees them. This is not the same as recognizing someone's face; by recognizing the fundamental error in the mind, one is freed from it and attains realization. In the practice of mindfulness, a certain degree of volition is needed at first. This mindfulness must first be created and then gradually transformed into the mindfulness of Dharmata.*

But still, people have thought patterns that obscure their natural state. In meditation they just replace these conceptions and habits with others that they call meditation. How does one get beyond meditations that are just replacements for conceptions?

Meditation without habits must be created on the basis of habits. If you are sharpening a knife and you keep on grinding it after it is sharp, you will eventually grind both knife and grindstone away. By creating the habit of watching the mind, one builds a habit of one-pointedness. At that stage there is something being watched and something watching. If one continues to watch and to be aware that something is watching and something else is being watched, gradually it will seem that both the watching and the watched vanish. At that moment, they both disappear in the fundamental nature. They disappear in Dharmata, and the resulting condition is meditation without habits.

When one begins meditating, a conception watches a conception, and as a result both of them disappear in the fundamental nature. When praying to Guru Rinpoche, one visualizes him in front of oneself, and when the prayer is finished, one imagines him dissolving into light and being absorbed into oneself. One becomes inseparable from him, as if both Guru Rinpoche and oneself were disappearing. This is another example of the mindfulness of Dharmata beyond conceptions. One should not think that it would take almost forever to attain this insight, as it would

*The mindfulness of Dharmata is mindfulness of the pure nature.

in the case of the knife and the grindstone being ground into nothing. Perhaps the collapse will occur at once, perhaps only after a lot of meditation practice—it is impossible to say.

There are other methods the teacher can use to show the nature of mind to the disciple. Could you describe some of the ways the teacher can show the disciple the fundamental nature in Mahamudra and Dzogchen?

There are many ways to introduce the nature of mind. In initiations, the Lama holds up a crystal, and this is the pointing out by sign. He is not just playing with the crystal; he is using it to show the nature of mind. At the same time, he gives an introduction to the nature of mind through words. Alcohol and a picture of the consort are also given in initiation; these are further introductions to the nature of mind by sign. In ancient literature, many other means of introducing the nature of mind are mentioned; indeed there are so many that it is impossible to impose an exact method for it or to give any all-inclusive account. Sometimes the introduction is given very subtly, sometimes it is given in a very obvious fashion, and sometimes it is given in the form of successive meditation instructions. Sometimes, as in the case of Naropa, it is given an aggressive expression. Tilopa said to Naropa, "Look at yourself—I have nothing to show you." Then he hit him over the head with a shoe, and Naropa attained insight. Yeshe Tsogyal gave the introduction of the nature of mind to seven rapists while they were raping her. This was an introduction of mind given through desire. These men had an extremely aggressive attitude toward her, but as she had great bodhichitta, she responded not with aggression but by introducing the nature of mind, enabling the rapists to attain realization.

So if you want to attain realization through desire, you have to look for a consort. If you want to attain it through aggression, you have to look for a fierce Lama. One can never predict how an indication of the nature of mind will occur, for this always depends on the Lama. Some teachers send their disciples away to practice meditation and ask afterward what problems arose. They try and clear away these problems and then send them back to do more meditation. This goes on for a few days or a few weeks or a few months or even a few years—the disciple repeatedly goes to the Lama and tells him about his meditation, and the Lama repeatedly clears up the disciple's meditation problems. Most Lamas teach in this fashion today, although a few still use the same method as Tilopa did, establishing the disciple in the right view at once, with no preparations.

By meditating, one can benefit a vast number of people. Great qualities can be developed through meditation, and even if a meditator seems very simple, he may have developed many profound qualities. With the development of meditation, one may be able to benefit people by teaching them Dharma. Even if one cannot teach much, one may perhaps be able to give a little advice about the preliminary practices. When you return to the West, you may be able to benefit your old friends and members of your family by talking to them about Dharma and about meditation. But do not hope to benefit rich businessmen and politicians who are too absorbed in their own concerns and are beyond being helped. If you try to help them, they will probably just get angry with you.

One can examine things or not, just as one pleases. If one is going to examine Dharma, one should examine it as one examines gold. In the East, people test gold by cutting it, scoring it, and rubbing it against a stone to see if it is pure. Just as one examines gold, so one should examine Dharma to see if it is the truth or not. This was what the Buddha said, and this statement is often repeated in justification of examining a lot of things from a Dharma point of view. It is also quoted by some Tibetans as a criticism of the Nyingmapas' tendency not to examine things. This same reference is quite often cited by the Gelugpas in justification of their intellectual approach to Dharma. This is standard in all Gelug commentaries, and any Gelug Lama will certainly uphold this point of view. But Longchen Rabjam gave a different interpretation of this statement. He said that examining Dharma does not refer to examining the teachings themselves at all, but means examining oneself. What one should examine is one's own nature in relation to the teachings. Dharma is the teaching of the Buddha, pure in itself, and there is no need to examine it. What one has to examine is one's own nature, to see what is applicable to oneself and how one can approach the teachings. Can one approach the Hinayana? Can one approach the Mahayana? Can one approach the Vajrayana? How will one be able to approach them? What one really has to examine is one's own character, one's own nature. Longchen Rabjam said that examining the teachings in the sense of examining different traditions in search of a pure teaching was not the original significance of the statement, but a later accretion.

None of this is intended as a criticism of anybody, but people of different traditions have come here today to see what kind of ideas I have. I do not really know very much about anything, and I have only said what I happen to think. I know how to be a politician and control what is said in order to please the audience, to take a politically correct approach, but I do not like doing that. I would rather just say what I think. If people like it, they like it; and if they do not like it, they do not. You should examine your mind, but not day and night. If you try to examine it day and night, you will just go crazy.

You gave an example of the introduction of the nature of mind through aggression. Could you give an example of an indication through ignorance?

There is no way the nature of mind can be introduced through ignorance. Ignorance is ignorance. If ignorance means failure to recognize something, how can it be used for recognition?

If the introduction of the nature of mind cannot be given through ignorance, how can it be given through desire and aggression? They come from ignorance, so they must also be of the nature of ignorance.

Do not think that ignorance is in any sense fundamental. Ignorance is like a cloud temporarily obscuring the sun but not inherent to the sky, and ignorance can vanish just like a cloud. In recognizing the fundamental nature of mind, one sees things as they are and there is no ignorance. On the path, ignorance should be considered lack of recognition of emptiness as the primordial characteristic of phenomena.

In meditation, two different approaches are sometimes indicated. One is to relax the mind and the other is to examine it. Do these really refer to different approaches, or are they just different descriptions of the same thing?

One technique involves looking for some self-nature in the skandhas. First one examines form. One examines the body to see if a mind or a self can be found in any part of the body: in the head, in the torso, in the feet, and so on. Then one examines the feelings—good, bad, and indifferent feelings—to see if a mind or self can be found there. In the same way, one examines perception, intention, and consciousness to try and find a self or real nature. This is called the analytical meditation method of the scholar. In the other technique, an advanced teacher gives a particular instruction on the nature of meditation to his disciples. In this method the analytical method is not used; the disciple leaves his mind in its natural condition without doing anything to it. This is called the yogi's method of leaving things as they are.

When you were talking about Mahayana, you mentioned looking at fundamental awareness when perceiving appearances. Does this involve investigation?

In Mahayana,* all appearances are visualized as Buddhafields and deities, all sounds are heard as mantras, and all conceptions are recognized to be of the nature of enlightenment. Once this meditation has been established, one does not carry out any more investigations.

When you have examined the five skandhas and seen the absence of self, what do you do next?

Nagarjuna and Atisha both said that the supreme finding is not finding anything at all, and the supreme seeing is not seeing anything at all. That is the whole point; that is what you are trying to find.

---

*In this case, the Mahayana refers to Vajrayana being classified together with the Bodhisattvayana as the Mahayana.

9 · Aspects of Buddhahood

Kaya, or aspect of Buddhahood, has two modes: Buddhahood as it is in itself, or Dharmakaya, and the expressive aspect, or Rupakaya. The Rupakaya itself has two aspects, Sambhogakaya and Nirmanakaya. The support of these two modes is the Dharmakaya, without which there could never be any expression of the Rupakaya. The expression of the Nirmanakaya is dependent upon the expression of the Sambhogakaya, which in turn is dependent upon the Dharmakaya. So without the Dharmakaya there could be no Sambhogakaya, and without the Sambhogakaya there could be no Nirmanakaya.

The Sambhogakaya is a nondual mode of expression in terms of characteristics, the natural expression of the Dharmakaya or the aspect of realization as it is in itself. There are two distinct traditions of teachings concerning the Sambhogakaya. In the Sutra tradition of a Sambhogakaya field a distinction is seen between the Teacher and the surrounding retinue relating to the center. In this case the principal Teacher is seen as a fully enlightened Buddha, and all the surrounding retinue are Bodhisattvas of the tenth level. In the tantras the Sambhogakaya is seen as entirely and utterly inseparable from the Dharmakaya. It is the natural expression of the Dharmakaya and has never left it even for a moment. There is no distinction between the minds of the surrounding deities and the central deity.

The Sambhogakaya is always considered utterly pure, but in the Nirmanakaya both aspects of purity and impurity are found; the Nirmanakaya can appear equally to a pure individual or to an impure individual. In the Nyingma tantras, as mentioned earlier, the Dharmakaya is described as endowed with two purities: the essentially and primordially pure Buddha nature, and the freedom from sudden stains in pure Buddhahood.

In the tantras the natural expression of the Sambhogakaya appears as a central deity and a retinue essentially inseparable from him: a Buddha expressing the final realized nature to surrounding disciples who are essentially inseparable from him. This expression does not depend on any effort, inclination, or impetus on the part of the Buddha, but is a natural activity of the nature of realization. Therefore, the transmission of Dharma initiates as a natural expression of inherent realization.

In the sutras, the tenth level is a Buddhafield where Bodhisattvas receive the final instructions from the Buddha, still perceived as somewhat separate from them. An individual not free from samsara would be unable to reach even the first level of Bodhisattvahood; but these beings are not only free from samsara, they are also purified of almost all their stains of conceptuality and have come close to the final realization of Buddhahood. In this condition they perceive a totally realized individual from whom they receive the teachings. Since they are already free from samsara, they have no further need of the Hinayana teachings, so teachings on this level are entirely Mahayana.

In the Mahayana, the structure of the Sambhogakaya is described in terms of five certainties. These are the place, time, teacher, retinue, and teaching. The certainty of place refers to the highest Buddhafield. In the pure perception of the tenth level, the Bodhisattvas perceive the abode of the highest Buddhafield. This is an extremely pure form of perception totally unlike the impure modes of perception of those who have not reached this level. The second certainty is concerned with time experience. In the ordinary, impure world we are caught in a time structure with a past and a future, a yesterday and a tomorrow and a day after tomorrow, and so on. The Bodhisattvas on the highest level are not involved in this structure. They experience a perpetual turning of the wheel of Dharma, the perpetual teaching and expression of enlightenment, until they attain realization. The third certainty is the teacher who expresses the teachings. In the sutras this is described as the five Buddhas expressing the various wisdoms of enlightenment,* while in

*Enlightened body, Buddha Vairochana of the Tathagata family; enlightened speech, Buddha Amitabha of the Padma family; enlightened mind, Buddha Akshobhya of the Vajra family; enlightened qualities, Buddha Ratnasambhava of the Ratna family; and enlightened activities, Buddha Amoghasiddhi of the Karma family.

the tantras the highest teacher is Dorje Chang [Vajradhara]. The fourth certainty is the retinue. In the sutras this does not mean ordinary individuals but refers to all those who have freed themselves from suffering and attained the tenth level of Bodhisattvahood, while in the tantras the retinue and the Buddha are not considered separable. The fifth certainty, the teaching, means the teaching of the Mahayana, because individuals at the tenth level of Bodhisattvahood are entirely of a Bodhisattva character, and so the Bodhisattva teachings are the most appropriate to them.

The Nirmanakaya has five uncertain aspects. The first of these is the uncertainty of the place. There is no particular place in which the Nirmanakaya expresses itself; it may do so wherever and in whatever form is necessary for the training of sentient beings. A Nirmanakaya aspect may appear in the hells, in the ghost realm, in the human realm, in the god realm, and so on. There is no absoluteness about where the Nirmanakaya may appear. There is similarly no absoluteness about the time at which a Nirmanakaya aspect may manifest itself. The Nirmanakaya aspect of the Buddha nature expresses itself whenever an individual sentient being is karmically ready to hear the teachings. If the individual relating to the Nirmanakaya is not ready, he may not perceive a teacher teaching him anything. Only if the karma of the individual is ripe for receiving the instructions will the Nirmanakaya appear to him and give him the appropriate teachings. This is like the reflection of the sun or the moon in water. If there are a number of pools or lakes or buckets or cups of water, there will be a sun or moon in each one; but if there is no water, there can be no reflection. So with beings, if their minds are ready, they will perceive the Nirmanakaya expressing the path to them. The third factor is the teacher. In terms of the Sambhogakaya, there is some certainty to the mode of appearance of the teacher, either as the five Buddhas or as Dorje Chang, but in Nirmanakaya terms there is no absoluteness about how a teacher will appear. There are many ways in which the Nirmanakaya can manifest as the teacher, but these can be summed up in three categories: the supreme manifestation of the Nirmanakaya, the created manifestation, and the born manifestation. The supreme manifestation is exemplified by Buddha Shakyamuni, who appears in the world expressing all the attributes of the Nirmanakaya in himself and performing the twelve deeds of a fully realized Buddha.* The created manifestations consist of objects that benefit sentient beings, such as thangkas or images of realized beings, and even such things as bridges and boats. The Nirmanakaya also manifests as all kinds of sentient beings to benefit different individuals. It manifests as different kinds of animals, as spiritual friends, as prostitutes, as businessmen, painters, men, women, people of high and of low position—it manifests in all manner of ways to help beings. Some people today feel that Nirmanakaya, or *tulku* in Tibetan, primarily means someone who sits on a throne and teaches Dharma, but this is not necessarily the case. The Nirmanakaya is completely non-absolute in its modes of expression and may express itself anywhere, at any time, in any form, to benefit beings.

It is not actually proper for me to teach while drinking tea, but there is no way out of it here. Tibetans are very fond of tea. In the old days people would bring a gigantic pot of tea and keep pouring from it during the teachings. During long periods of instruction this would create an obvious problem, so the students would keep a urinary vessel under their seat. If they needed to urinate, they would hold it under their robes and urinate while listening to the teachings, then seal it up and put it back underneath their seat. This is an old Tibetan custom, but it seems to be dying out now.

The fourth non-absolute factor of the Nirmanakaya is the uncertainty of the retinue, or the people taught by the manifestations. In the Sutra tradition the Sambhogakaya manifests only to tenth-level Bodhisattvas, but the Nirmanakaya manifests to very impure beings as well. It manifests to people who practice Dharma, to ordinary people who have no Dharma, and even to very evil people who are completely against Dharma or who greatly harm sentient beings. We saw that the Sambhogakaya expresses only the Mahayana teachings because of the nature of the individuals being taught, but the Nirmanakaya manifestations give all kinds of teach-

*The twelve deeds (mdzad pa bcu gnyis) are: descending from Tushita, entering the mother's womb, taking rebirth, becoming expert in all arts, enjoying circles of queenly consorts, having renunciation and taking ordination, engaging in austerities for six years, sitting under the bodhi tree, annihilating hordes of demons, approaching the essence of enlightenment, turning the wheel of Dharma, and passing into mahaparinirvana.

ing to all kinds of individuals. They teach the Hinayana, the Mahayana, and the Vajrayana under different circumstances to different individuals.

Which of the Three Kayas would Guru Rinpoche be?

That depends on how you approach Guru Rinpoche. If one is doing a Guru Rinpoche practice and approaching him in his Nirmanakaya aspect, he is a Nirmanakaya expression. If one approaches him in his Sambhogakaya aspect, he is the Sambhogakaya, and if one approaches him in his Dharmakaya aspect, he is the Dharmakaya. The Sambhogakaya great compassion aspect of Padmasambhava is Chenrezig, with many expressions in terms of the five families, and the Dharmakaya aspect is Boundless Light.*

Which of the three aspects of the Nirmanakaya would he be?

There are eight Nirmanakaya aspects of Padmasambhava, some of them siddhas and others supernormal forms, each with a different name. One could consider Padmasambhava as expressing all types of Nirmanakaya manifestation. In the *Nirvana Sutra,* Buddha Shakyamuni said that one hundred and twelve years after he left the world he would return in a superior form. This referred to Padmasambhava. It shows that he was not in any way different from Buddha Shakyamuni and that he can therefore be considered a supreme manifestation. Of the eight forms of Padmasambhava, Shakya Seng-ge is that which is the same as Buddha Shakyamuni. In the life of Padmasambhava, there are accounts of his making various images and engaging in other crafts. Some of these he seemed to make with his own hands, others he manifested supernormally. These were all created manifestations.

All the Buddhas are inherent in and are described by the aspects of the Three Kayas; or from another point of view, all the Buddhafields and all of enlightenment are pervaded by the aspects of the Three Kayas and defined by them. These Three Kayas can be described in terms of the five Buddha families, the five wisdoms, and the Five Kayas. The Five Kayas represent a specifically tantric system of describing enlightenment, while the Sutra tradition refers mainly to Three or Four Kayas. In general, all

*Buddha Amitabha.

Buddhas and all Buddhist deities can be considered from the point of view of the Three Kayas, and this is the most general system. The Hinayana, however, does not refer to the Three Kayas, the five certainties, or the five uncertain aspects of the Nirmanakaya. It is important to understand the systems used within the different vehicles and not to confuse them.

I have been asked to talk about the five Buddha families as they relate to the Five Kayas and the five wisdoms. This is a Vajrayana approach to the nature of realization but does not contradict the Mahayana approach, although the Mahayana does not normally speak in those terms. The Mahayana teachings are vast, however, and in one or two Mahayana scriptures the five families are nonetheless mentioned, and the Dharmakaya, Sambhogakaya, and Nirmanakaya plus the Svabhavikakaya, or Essence Kaya, which is the Three Kayas as indivisible, not distinct from the other three. This is an involved topic on which much has been written, but in brief the Three Kayas are not independent things but aspects of the same essence. The essence of the three aspects undivided is the Svabhavikakaya. The Vajrayana also refers to a fifth aspect, the Vajrakaya or aspect of actual enlightenment, which means the perfect expression of all the qualities of the enlightened nature.*

The five families as aspects of realization are the Tathagata family, which is enlightened body; the Padma family, enlightened speech; the Vajra family, enlightened mind; the Ratna family, enlightened qualities; and the Karma family, enlightened activities. The five wisdoms are the wisdom of Dharmadhatu; discerning wisdom; mirrorlike wisdom; the wisdom of equanimity; and all-accomplishing wisdom. These definitions of the wisdoms and the families are not mutually exclusive; rather they are indications of predominant characteristics. The Tathagata family, for example, not only expresses enlightened body but points to a mode of expression in which that characteristic is more central. All five characteristics are present in any one of the families. This can be further understood by considering the ways in which ordinary people express themselves. This example is not strictly applicable because there is no way a Buddha's qualities can be compared to those of an ordinary sentient

*In *A Cascading Waterfall of Nectar*, Kyabje Thinley Norbu Rinpoche gives the Vajrakaya as another name for the fourth Kaya, which is one system; here another system is used, in which Vajrakaya is the fifth Kaya.

being, but without examples it is difficult for us to gain any understanding of the nature of realization. Some people, then, seem to be predominantly physical in their expression. They might be very beautiful or strong, or concern themselves a great deal with their bodies. Others have a predominantly verbal mode of expression; their natural field of influence is greatest through their voice and through verbal communication. In yet other people the intellectual mode of expression is foremost; they concern themselves principally with their own thought processes. In some people, none of these three factors predominates, although they may have qualities that are essentially expressive and that come out in different ways in their lives. Other people express themselves principally through their activities and their work; in this case their expression is less something personal to them than something involved with their activities. People have different ways of expressing themselves, but they all have a body, speech, mind, qualities, and activities. These five characteristics of ordinary human beings do not correspond at all to the five aspects of Buddhahood, but there is some correspondence in the sense that although one of them might predominate, all are invariably present.

I described earlier the various ways of choosing the deity one is going to practice, but in very rough terms one can see what kind of deity is appropriate just by examining one's own character. A person largely dominated by stupidity would incline toward the practices of the Tathagata family. One largely dominated by desires might best benefit by practicing a deity of the Padma family to develop discerning wisdom. Someone largely dominated by aversion would be suited to practicing a deity of the Vajra family to develop mirrorlike wisdom; someone largely dominated by pride would be suited to practicing a deity of the Ratna family to develop the wisdom of equanimity; and someone largely dominated by jealousy would be suited to practicing a deity of the Karma family.

Even though our understanding of the nature of realization and the Five Kayas may be incomplete, if we turn the mind in on itself and watch our own nature, we will recognize that these Five Kayas, five wisdoms, and five families are all contained within our own nature. Nothing in the fundamental nature of the mind can be shown to be conceptual. This is the Dharmakaya aspect within us. This fundamental condition beyond conceptuality is not merely empty, but naturally expressive as brilliant light. It is neither substantial nor independently existent, and in no sense other than the fundamental Dharmakaya nature. This natural expressiveness, inseparable from the Dharmakaya nature, is the Sambhogakaya aspect of our nature. If we leave the mind alone, as it is, without doing anything to it, without creating or distorting anything in it, we will recognize that the mind itself is unobstructed. This unobstructed quality is the foundation of compassion, and the very meaning of compassion is unobstructedness. This is the Nirmanakaya aspect of realization in our nature.

With sufficient faith in the nature of the mind, it is possible to attain this realization spontaneously, but according to Tibetan tradition a lineage and an instructor are necessary to recognition of the fundamental nature, and for this reason it is necessary to develop a relationship with a realized Lama and receive the blessings of the lineage.

The Vajrayana holds that in leaving the mind as it is, receiving the blessings of the lineage, and recognizing the fundamental nature through the Lama's teachings, one is already inherently realized, already inherently a Buddha. This is the Tathagata family in one's own nature. In the sutras it is said only that Buddhahood is potential in every individual; but according to the tantras, all beings are already Buddhas.

In recognizing the fundamental nature, one impartially recognizes all the expressions of samsara as enlightened. One recognizes the needs of all beings and understands all facets of Dharma. One develops great potential to express Dharma oneself and acquires control over the power of speech. This faculty is the Padma family in one's own nature.

By leaving the mind alone without distorting it, one can also realize that no quality could ever benefit one and no flaw could ever harm one. This recognition of the fundamental sameness of everything is immutable, like a vajra. *Vajra* does not mean the thing with lots of prongs on it that people wave around in ceremonies; that is only the symbol of the vajra. The real vajra is the immutable quality of sameness, and recognizing this sameness is the Vajra family in one's fundamental nature.

This natural condition of mind also enables one to recognize that all events, qualities, and phenomena are merely an expression of mind. One therefore develops a profound confidence in the nature of these phenomena and recognizes that there is nothing in them to which one can become attached. *Ratna* means "jewel." This is a metaphorical usage, and metaphors are always necessary in communication. A jewel is generally quite small, but nonetheless it has many special properties such as refracting light and, in Tibetan belief, counteracting poisons, and is therefore considered valuable. Recognizing the fundamental nature itself and understanding that it has no substantiality, seeing that all phenomena and all qualities arise from it, is the Ratna family in one's own nature.

The fundamental nature is naturally expressive of totality, and this totality is perceived without error, confusion, or attachment. There is no duality, and one has effortless control over any situation. This freedom effortlessly manifests Buddha activities, with the freedom from attachment to the effortless manifestation of the fundamental nature recognized as it is. This is the karma family in one's own nature.

Recognizing the fundamental nature is perception of the Dharmadhatu. *Dhatu* means "space," not in the sense of physical space, but metaphorically—the mind of all the Buddhas. This is like space in that it is extremely vast, extremely profound, boundless, and unobstructed. In perceiving this space of the Buddha mind, one perceives the wisdom of the Dharmadhatu in one's own nature.

Given the blessings of the lineage and the appropriate instructions from the Lama, one can recognize the mirrorlike quality of the fundamental nature by leaving the mind without distortion. In the recognition of this natural clarity, one no longer clings to a self. One ceases to create duality, and instead of wandering in the confusion of ignorance one remains in the clarity and brilliance of the fundamental nature. If one does not become distracted by the arising of phenomena or allow the mind to be controlled by them but continues to look at the fundamental nature, all outer conditions become irrelevant. Whether they are bad or good is immaterial, since one does not take a judgmental attitude toward them. This is the wisdom of sameness in one's own nature. When one leaves the mind as it is, turning it in toward itself and recognizing the fundamental nature, outer appearances arise by themselves, unmixed. One does not discriminate any shape or color, any specific thisness or thatness, any separate thingness about anything in the world, but constantly recognizes the fundamental nature. This does not obstruct the arising of appearances. Visual appearances and sounds continue to arise in one's field of consciousness, unmixed, unconfused, as they are. This is discerning wisdom in one's own nature. When one leaves the mind in its basic nature, all appearances arise as an expression of emptiness, inseparable from it. This active aspect of emptiness is total potential.* All appearances arise as the activity of emptiness, effortlessly and without one's having to do anything about it. This is Buddha activity in one's own basic nature.

This is only the briefest of introductions to the five families, the five wisdoms, and the Three or Five Kayas. To go beyond this would involve a description of the qualities of the Five Kayas and the five families, which is an enormous topic. The entire scope of Dharma and the very nature of realization can be described in terms of the Five Kayas. We could spend our whole lives studying them and still not get to the end. If we look outward and try to learn about things, we will never reach the end because learning is endless.

I have described how to recognize the five Buddha families in your own nature. I have not said that you have all realized them already or that there is nothing more to do. They still have to be recognized. Once having recognized them, it is important to continue meditating on the fundamental nature and to develop the full experience of its recognition. The nature of the Tathagata family is unobstructedness and non-fogginess. One must keep awareness clear, the fundamental awareness of the basic nature. This is the manner of practicing the wisdom of the Dharmadhatu.

When pride arises, do not be controlled by it; return to the recognition of the fundamental awareness. Pride can be very gross, as one can see in arrogant people, or it can take a subtle form that is felt inwardly but does not have a strong outward manifestation. It is important to recognize pride at the moment of its arising. When one has recognized it, one should neither follow nor control it, but return to the condition of awareness. Pride will suddenly disappear together with its object—some knowledge or skill with which one identifies—and what will be left will be the wisdom of equanimity. One can make use of pride.

One should not take feelings of unhappiness, pain, depression, excitement, and happiness as anything real. As soon as these feelings arise, one

*That is, "the readiness to reflect anything," as Kyabje Thinley Norbu Rinpoche would say.

should refer to fundamental awareness, rather than becoming attached to them. One will recognize that all conditions, no matter how unhappy or happy, bad or good, are endowed with the one taste of the fundamental nature. This practice of one taste is the realization of the wisdom of sameness.

One can make use of desire. If one sees something very attractive, such as a beautiful woman, the mind automatically becomes attached and one feels desire. At this point it is very important not to allow the mind to become controlled by attachment, but to turn it in on itself and recognize the fundamental nature. One will then cease to create any duality of self and object and will therefore cease to be attached. Desires will automatically disappear, and discerning wisdom will arise in their place. If a woman saw a handsome man, she would automatically feel desire for him. At the point of recognizing that desire, it is important to turn the mind in on itself and recognize the fundamental nature. All appearances and the very notion of self and other will become mixed in a single unitary expression, and there will be no dual structure. Desire itself will disappear, and what will be left is discriminating wisdom. This applies also to men being attracted to women. I am not making any recommendations whatever about sexual activity one way or the other. There is no particular reason for avoiding sexual activity if one has some purpose or some practice to use it for.

It is far better to watch the mind than to repress anything. Repressing a desire only makes it arise again. One will forever be repressing it, and this constant repression will lead to mental disease. It is far better just to watch the mind, to watch the fundamental nature in accordance with the instructions of the Lama. In recognizing the nature of the mind, all appearances become integrated in sole oneness and are seen as they are.

Such meditations can often be very useful. When one feels attracted to a member of the opposite sex, it does not always follow that this feeling is reciprocated, and one often finds oneself in frustrating circumstances. If one knows how to meditate, one loses one's attachment and the situation does not cause any trouble. One does not need to masturbate or go madly chasing around in circles, and so the practice can even be useful.

With this attitude, potentially frustrating situations never cause any difficulties. Even if two people are very attached to one another, all phenomena in samsara are impermanent, and although a relationship may be temporarily happy, it can lead to suffering. One of the partners may die, or the couple may be separated. So at the time of feeling attachment and desire, it is important to leave the mind in the fundamental nature, to recognize the fundamental nature and see things as they are. In this way, one will not become confused by desires and attachments. If circumstances bring about separation from one's husband, wife, or lover, one experiences no difficulties with the mind. If one has recognized the wisdom of sameness and discriminating wisdom by habitually referring to the fundamental nature in happy conditions, one will not go crazy over suffering.

Whether as a result of attitudes based on education, attitudes toward members of the opposite sex, or envy of another's fame or reputation, people sometimes feel jealous of others. At the moment jealousy first arises, it is very important to watch the nature of the mind. This observation of its arousal will make the jealousy particularly strong, but one should never be confused by this, and never follow the jealous impulse. Never allow the jealous impulse to make you sarcastic, aggressive, or bitter, even for a moment. It will arise in your mind very strongly, but if you keep your reference to the fundamental nature and remain without doing anything, without confusing anything in your mind, you will experience no duality, and the energy of jealousy will spontaneously become all-accomplishing wisdom, the activities of all Buddhas.

People from Central Tibet, and Eastern people in general, have similar cultural conditioning to that of the English and French in that they try to maintain a degree of propriety. When they feel impulses of jealousy or aggression, their propriety makes them keep these feelings inside. Even when their emotions are very strong, they are skilled at never allowing them to be shown. Do not do this. Americans, on the other hand, tend to express jealousy and aggression the moment these feelings arise—by grabbing someone and beating him up, for example. One should not do this either. When jealousy and other such feelings arise in the mind, watch them, watch the mind, and do not be confused by these feelings. Neither bottle them up nor blow them up. Watch the mind, watch the fundamental nature, and natural wisdom will arise. It is said in Madhyamaka that if one abides in no extreme, wisdom will arise by itself. If one abides neither in the extreme of eternalism nor in the extreme of nihilism but leaves the mind just as it is, wisdom will arise by itself. If one abides in neither the Eastern extreme nor the American extreme, the wisdom beyond the extremes of East and West will arise.

I have been asked again and again to give Dzogchen teachings, but to do this the teacher himself must first have a high development of wisdom. I am not in this position. Furthermore, Dzogchen is in a sense an elaborate matter. Very high levels of understanding are involved, and I have neither the grasp of that understanding nor any of the other great qualities that a Dzogchen teacher must have. Then, the disciples must have taken the appropriate initiation. Although I have not examined the situation, I feel that a good number of you may not have the specific Dzogchen initiation, and for these reasons I have not approached the teachings of Dzogchen as such. Nonetheless, some of you want to hear something about Dzogchen and so I have tried to say a few things that are beneficial on the Dzogchen path.

Sectarian differences have always existed in Buddhism. In ancient India there were sectarian differences between Hinayana and Mahayana. Later on, distinctions arose between the four schools, and in Tibet differences grew between the four sects. These differences did not occur because of any flaw in Dharma but rather because of faults in beings' minds. What one must do in Dharma is maintain an attitude of discipline toward the mind in harmony with the Hinayana, a calm condition of mind in harmony with the Mahayana, and a feeling of the pure perception of all appearances in harmony with the Vajrayana. These are the three most essential factors in Dharma practice, and even if one is not able to practice Dharma at every moment, these attitudes will be of great benefit.

10 · Tantra in Action

When involved in Dharma and relating to Lamas, watch the condition of your mind. Many people go through radical changes when studying and practicing Dharma. When they approach a great Lama, their minds become fixed, hard, and rather aggressive, and they seem principally concerned with declaring their own positive qualities. Because of these emotional reactions, their minds become tight and closed in, they get wrapped up in their own concerns, and in this state they are unable to benefit sentient beings. When they do have the impulse to benefit others, they select prominent individuals and totally ignore ordinary people. Although it is no fault of the Lamas themselves, people do tend to create this sort of situation in the company of great Lamas. With a rigid attitude, it is impossible to have real faith in the Lama, and without that faith we cannot benefit other beings. It is vital to watch the mind and keep it open and relaxed.

An open mind is also important in studying Dharma. We should never feel that we have gotten hold of something or understood it completely. We should keep an open mind and avoid fixed concepts. Otherwise, study will just make us constricted and will become an obstacle.

The best way to approach a Lama is to keep an open and relaxed mind and develop the perception of the Lama as very pure. If we take this attitude and are open about ourselves, we will be able to establish clear contact with the Lama, free of any adulteration from our own mind's orientation. We will have no feelings such as "I am this Lama's disciple" or "This Lama is better than any other Lama." Heavy conceptions of this sort just will not arise. But without a relaxed approach it is easy to develop these defiled attitudes—I am probably subject to them myself, they arise so readily. Certainly I noticed them a good deal in Europe, particularly among people in the inner circle of prominent Lamas. People who associate with those Lamas but are not so close to them do not seem to develop such faults to the same degree.

People who are studying a religion are often critical of others. They put people down and treat them badly. Why do you think they do this?

Jealousy.

Do you think that is a sufficient explanation?

Insecurity. Dualistic mind.

How could it be dualistic mind?

I don't know, I never understood that teaching.

Dualistic in the sense that you are trying to become something, trying to become established in something strong, and the ego is grasping at it.

How could we end all this? The Buddha came into the world and did not manage to end it, so it is unlikely that we will ever be able to do so. But supposing we tried, how would we go about it?

Make more offerings.

What kind of offerings do you want to make—chocolate cakes?

Everyone could start by cutting off their little finger and take it from there.

You mean you want to offer your physical body?

Figuratively, not literally.

How would offering your own body destroy duality? It sounds more like suicide to me.

That's why I said figuratively, not literally. I have a lot of very gross dualistic conceptions that usually center on my body; I tend to identify with it.

Isn't that like placing your target in the west and shooting your arrows to the east?

It's always like that. You shoot in one direction, and it's probably going to be wrong because it's based on delusion. All thoughts are influenced by the ego.

But is there any real need ever to offer anything? Anything you might see as external to yourself is merely a creation of your own mind. If you forget about objectifying a realm and look at the nature of your own mind, doesn't that destroy any object you could ever concretize?

I appreciate intellectually that there is no inherent reality in any object, but at this stage it has been easier for me to make offerings of myself, my delusions, and everything I value. I don't know if it makes any real difference, but this is a feeling I have. Of course, I know it is not really possible to make any kind of offering, but it eases my mind.

Making offerings is certainly beneficial to the mind, but what are you going to do about negativity? Are you going to cut a finger off every time you become proud or start getting angry with someone? Are you going to start making ritual offerings of tormas? Maybe you won't be able to find enough coloring, flour, and butter to make them. Are you going to carry all these tormas around with you everywhere you go so that you can make offerings every time it seems necessary?

No, what I'd rather do is offer the energy. I see pride as the energy of habits arising in me. When it arises, or when sexual energy or any other sort of energy arises in me, I make offerings of it. So whatever happens, I try to be mindful and offer the energy in the same way as I would offer tormas.

How are you going to offer this pride?

Well, as I see it, pride isn't really a thing. It's just a feeling that arises when someone gives me a compliment, for instance. Suddenly it's there—it arises so quickly that often I'm not aware of it. This energy isn't really there—it's not an actual thing—but it's a strong energy, strong enough to take me by surprise. So I offer this energy of pride that grows in me so quickly, and I try to give it to something else.

If you see that pride itself is not of the nature of pride, what need is there to go any farther? If pride doesn't have any force of its own, there is no need to cut your finger off or make any other offerings. If you realize that pride doesn't have any prideness, there is nowhere else to go.

I have not reached a conscious and stable realization of the absolute nature of pride or the other defilements. I know it intellectually, but sometimes I get carried away. Last night I was sitting meditating and I noticed sexual energy arising, so I decided to observe it and see what would happen, to try and understand its nature. Then I made an offering of it.

That is something like making an offering. If you recognize an impulse at the moment of its arising, it can be seen as inherently empty, and therefore destroyed. It is good to make offerings of ordinary impulses, but this still creates a vast number of additional conceptions leading to further births. It is far better to recognize an impulse at the moment of its arising and cut it off at that point. When cutting down a tree, it is best to cut at the root, for no matter how many branches are cut off, more will grow in their place.

Sooner or later you will all probably go back to the West. You will have to live there somehow or another—that is none of my business, and I am not going to ask how you are going to do it. But having come here and received a lot of teachings, you should try to benefit sentient beings. You should try to benefit people with what you have learned in the East. Although we do not know the future, if someone asked me how I was going to help beings when I got back to Bhutan, I could say what was on my mind at that moment. What is on your mind about how you can benefit beings in the West? How are you going to help people with what you have learned in the East?

Through the example of your own life. If you set a good example yourself, this will help others. But you shouldn't go around saying you're a Buddhist and you know a lot about the Dharma. That doesn't help. First let people appreciate the Dharma. Rejoice over their actions or show them their qualities without mentioning the Dharma, without saying "Buddhist."

How are you going to tell what are bad and good qualities in these people? It is very difficult to say what is unvirtuous and what is virtuous in somebody. If you do not know what aspirations sentient beings have, you cannot know how to benefit them. How are you going to benefit them if you do not know their aspirations?

Could you explain the four activities of pacifying, enriching, controlling, and destroying? How can they be used to benefit sentient beings?

The four activities are ordinary worldly forms of realization and are an excellent approach to this problem. Pacifying means pacifying all the things that cause suffering to sentient beings, such as diseases, unvirtuous actions, and bad conditions. Enabling people to build qualities or gain things they need is the activity of expanding or enriching. This activity helps beings to overcome poverty and want, to develop in the Dharma, and to develop wisdom. Controlling does not mean control through effort or trying to do anything; recognizing all seemingly external forms as a projection of the mind will bring them under our control. To experience phenomena as external is to be controlled by them. If everything is recognized as our own projection, all circumstances are effortlessly controlled. The fourth activity is destruction. Some individuals are incapable of being trained or benefited by any means, whether pacifying, enriching, or controlling, and when an individual falls into this category, only the activity of destroying is appropriate. In brief, pacifying demons, diseases, and sufferings is the activity of pacifying; enriching means increasing beings' wealth, development, and wisdom; controlling means not being controlled by external circumstances; and destroying means using destructive means to subdue pride and aggression when no other method can counteract these defilements.

You were saying that perhaps it is better not to try to teach Dharma, not to say that we are Buddhists, and so forth. Maybe this is a decision we do not have to take. If the time comes for us to say we are not involved in Dharma, we can recognize that moment and act accordingly. If that occasion does not occur, no matter how much we insist on the point, it will not benefit anybody.

It is very difficult to make any decision about what is going to benefit somebody. Some feel it is best to become monks or nuns in order to practice Dharma and benefit people, while others feel it is best not to take monastic ordination. Different people have different ideas on how best to approach benefiting people, and many of these ideas stem from karma and aspirations built up in previous lives.

It is very hard to make a decision about exactly what to do in the West, but perhaps we can make some sort of general indication. First of all, it is important always to sustain our meditation, no matter what tradition we follow or what our practice is. Then we should imitate the behavior of the people we relate to; in this way we can get close to others and benefit them. If we are with rigid people we should be rigid ourselves; if we are with people who are natural we should become very natural; and if we are with blunt people we should also be blunt. If we are open and relaxed with someone who is rigid, our attitude will terrify him because he will never be able to understand how a relaxed mind functions. He will become afraid and withdraw. We will not have any way to relate to him, and thus will not be able to benefit him. We should not be open and relaxed with rigid people. On the other hand, if we adopt a sharp or rigid approach to somebody open-minded and easygoing, we will fail to expand his qualities and so waste the opportunity of relating to him. In that case we should take an attitude similar to his own, and be open and easygoing ourselves.

But what if you are with people who smoke dope and drink a lot?

What you should do is get drunk or stoned with them for a few days to establish some basis for the association. If you meet a drunk and tell him straight off that it is no good to drink, he just will not want to hang around. He will leave and that will be the end of it. But if you drink with him for a few days, eventually one or both of you will get sick and then you will be able to say, "You know, it is not really good to drink so much. Somehow we've got to stop all this drinking."

When I try to do this, I usually end up getting so drunk or stoned I can't meditate. If I'm uptight with people who are uptight, I have a hard time cooling down and meditating. It all sounds very good, but it also sounds dualistic. I'm not sure if I can pull it off.

If you have doubts about your ability to function in any situation, it is better not to approach it. Keep functioning within whatever sphere is conducive to your meditation and try to benefit beings in that frame of reference.

When relating to people, it is very important not to be judgmental under any circumstances. If you happen to meet a thief or see someone stealing something, you should not immediately think, "He's a thief—this is terrible. He's a very bad person and he is creating a lot of bad karma." Neither should you criticize him for being a thief. That will just drive him away and will not do him any good. There is no reason for any of these ideas. Just keep a completely open mind.

Thieves are thieves because there is a law against stealing. If there were no law against it, a lot of people would steal and society would become chaotic. But in fact no one person steals any more or any less than any other. If we objectify an appearance and take it to be real, we have taken something that was not originally ours, or stolen something. In that sense everyone is a thief. If somebody goes out and picks up a few things that other people think are theirs, it does not make him any more of a thief than anyone else. So while we should not tell a thief that it is good to steal, there is no reason to pronounce a judgment on an individual just because he is a thief. Or if we saw a couple making love in a crowd, we might think they were rather ill-mannered, but there is no need for that judgment. We should just open our minds to everything and make no discriminations at all.

There is no reality in anything whatever. Everything is mere illusion, and nothing is any more or less real than anything else, so there is no need to make discriminations. Judgments alienate us from people, but if we are open-minded and nonjudging, we will be able to relate to people and benefit them. Extreme views automatically limit us. If we take too extreme a view of ethical standards, we may be able to benefit a few people through our belief and understanding, but we will be unable to benefit people through the correct view. If we have a strong feeling for the highest view of absolute truth and continually relate from that point of view, we will benefit people, but if we are contemptuous of ethical standards we will just drive away those who are attracted to them. So it is very important not to take any particular view and to adopt no position or judgment whatever.

If you ever return to the West, you will find many Dharma centers there, all with offices. Maintain an open attitude toward those offices. Do not be instantly critical of them. Look at them, see what the people are like there, what kind of unvirtuous and virtuous impulses they have, and what kind of development they have attained through contact with so many high Lamas. There are also places in the West where there is no Dharma at all, and if you go to these places, you should approach the local people with the same attitude and watch to see what kind of feelings they have. Having done this, you should ask yourself why people who have been practicing Dharma seem to have so many faults and why simple people who have never heard of Dharma often have so many good qualities. Why does this happen? Why is it that Dharma people have so many disturbing thoughts and such bad impulses, while a lot of people outside Dharma have fewer disturbing thoughts and better impulses?

Maybe it's because the karma of people who are practicing Dharma is ripening faster. It looks as if they are deteriorating, but in fact they are just getting rid of more bad karma. If you dust the corners, the room always looks dirtier than when you started.

It is usually easy to see if someone is practicing Dharma in this lifetime, but not so easy to say whether someone not practicing Dharma in this lifetime has practiced in previous lifetimes.

People who are not practicing Dharma now may have practiced in a former life, so now they seem very good; and the people who are practicing now are getting rid of all their bad karma because they did not practice in former lives.

On what basis do you make the decision that someone who looks as if he is more defiled is actually more pure?

I am not saying that he is pure, but perhaps his karma is ripening faster, so he is going through more negativity, and perhaps dealing with it in his practice.

Yes, but we are talking about the creation of karma, not its fruition. Dealing with someone's momentary impulses is karmically creative. We are trying to create pure impulses in practicing the Dharma, and trying to plant pure seeds to give growth to realization. The expression of defilement is not a question of something coming to fruition; it is a question of what is being created. To take an example, a farmworker's impulses may not be especially pure or good, but if they are not particularly negative, he will create less bad karma.

What is the process of purification? Does it mean that your negativity comes out?

What determines purification is our motivation. If we transform our motivation and constantly try to benefit beings, purification will actually occur. There is no real or necessary connection between motivation and action. Some people have very pure motivation, yet from the outside their actions may seem rough and impure. Others seem to act in a virtuous manner but have unvirtuous minds. Some people have basically impure minds, and this shows in everything they do; others have pure minds, and this also is expressed in all their actions. It is best if our motivation is completely pure and we can express this purity in action, but if this is not possible, motivation is most important. It is vital for us to transform our motivation, no matter what our actions are like.

When you go back to the West, just watch the show. Watch what goes on around you, and do not make any decisions or judgments at all. And as you watch, watch your mind. When you meet people involved in the Dharma, look at what they are like and watch your mind. When you meet ordinary people, watch them without making judgments, and watch your mind. When you go into the country, look at the people there, see how they are, and watch your mind. When you see qualities in people, examine those qualities without making any judgments about them and see why Dharma people have bad or good qualities and why other people have bad or good qualities. Do not make any judgments about people. If you approach the world in that way, you will get a new idea and a new feeling about things, and you will understand how to benefit the West.

We should also watch people's emotions, try to understand the nature of their unhappiness and happiness, and see where these come from. Some people seem to be happy but are in fact unhappy, and some seem as if they should be unhappy, yet they are not. Some people seem to be happy, but their happiness is leading them into suffering. A boxer would seem to be creating his own suffering by getting into the ring. He is going to get hit, and this definitely seems to cause suffering. But a boxer getting into the ring is not thinking about the suffering of getting hit; he is thinking about the money and how happy it will make him. That is why he gets into boxing. We should try to understand people's happiness and suffering in an ultimate sense. If we cannot do anything about their temporary happiness, it is best to forget about it, but we should try to lead people to happiness in an ultimate sense.

If we have a choice between helping one person and helping many, it is better to help many. If we have a choice between helping a good person and helping a bad person, it is better to help the bad one. Sometimes we have to defer a little to those in high positions in order to help ordinary people. In these circumstances, we have to give a little thought to important people, but otherwise we should think about benefiting ordinary individuals—we do not really have to pay much attention to important people.

It is very important to give up selective motivation and activity in our relations with people. There is nothing wrong in benefiting any specific individual, but we should avoid all selectivity in our motivation. If we avoid choosing whom we are going to benefit, give up selective ideas about individuals, and just work choicelessly, specific individuals will automatically be benefited. If our motivation is to benefit specific individuals, in the end we will never be able to benefit anyone.

Nowadays we all seem to be looking for fame and position, but we never get them. Even if one of us manages to become president, eventually he will lose the position and be forgotten. Trying to gain fame or position can be compared to advertising. As long as the idiotic message is constantly reiterated through the media, people will continue to think about the product; but as soon as the message stops, people will stop thinking about it. Fame and position are fickle. In ancient times there were a great many siddhas who were unknown in their own time but are now famous. They acted like ordinary individuals, went about their affairs, and practiced their meditation, never trying to get anything for themselves. Nonetheless, the force of their non-trying—the effortless manifestation of their realized nature—expressed itself so strongly that they have become well known today. If you want fame, give up fame. If you want a high position, give up all desire for it. If you do this, you will achieve everything you could want. You will gain power, but you will not be attached to it, and you will no longer create the source of samsara in yourself, so you will be able to benefit beings through your activities. All the Buddha's teachings can be summed up in the word "freedom." Freedom means freedom from suffering and freedom from samsara, and whatever frees beings from suffering and samsara is in accord with the teachings of Buddha.

There are both Tibetans and Westerners here this evening. I do not feel that one is any better than the other, and I have not been able to develop any of the good qualities of either. On the other hand, I have managed to develop the bad habits of both, and so I can get along well in the company of either. One has to work on developing one's faults in order to get some idea of what good qualities are. Many people have ideas such as "This monk is very pure. His ethics are impeccable, and he does not even know the ways of unvirtuous action, the ordinary ways of couples in love." This is contradictory. Although people try to praise even Buddha in this way, they only succeed in disparaging him. The omniscience of a Buddha means he knows all the bad as well as all the good. He may not express negativity, but he certainly knows it. In order to attain realization of nirvana, one must understand the ways of samsara. In order to develop positive qualities, one must start with understanding bad actions.

What bad things do you have to understand?

Stealing, killing, telling lies, cheating—there are lots of bad things you can understand. This way you will really understand what good is, and the worse these bad things are, the better you will understand positive qualities. If you never understand anything bad to begin with, you will never understand what good is. If I were sharing a room with someone I did not know, I would never get more than a vague idea of what he was like if I were good to him all the time. The best approach would be to anger him; then I would certainly find out what he was like. If he got furious with me, I would know that he was trying to cope with his aggression, and then I would be able to benefit him in some way. This would be the result of the initial anger I would cause him.

When living with Easterners, it is usually best to act like them, being slow and careful. But in the case of Westerners, particularly Americans, it is probably best to be aggressive from the start. Then one can see what they are like. This is because of the difference in habits between East and West. Westerners are generally speedy, and consequently an abrupt attitude is more suitable. There is no inherent superiority in being slow, and no inherent inferiority in being speedy; and when one approaches people, one should meet them on their own energy level. Meet speedy people with speed and relaxed people with a relaxed attitude. American speediness can be a positive quality, but it tends to be applied only to material things, not Dharma. On the other hand, speediness leads to an unstable attitude, and for this reason Americans often have difficulty progressing in Dharma. Eastern slowness can also be a positive quality, but being slow and relaxed all the time can lead to a fixed attitude.

How does Dorje Sempa practice purify your motivation? What does purification mean in Dorje Sempa practice?

Every Buddha attains Buddhahood as a result partly of his prayers of aspiration, and each realized individual has his own modes of aspiration. When Manjushri was on the Bodhisattva path, he prayed that all beings should attain realization. Since the prime reason beings wander in samsara is ignorance, he resolved to work to dispel their ignorance in whatever way he could. On attaining realization, he manifested a form dispelling all kinds of ignorance. For this reason, Manjushri is considered to be the deity of learning and knowledge in Buddhism. Similarly, when Dorje Sempa [Vajrasattva] was on the path, he felt that the prime reason for sentient beings' wandering in suffering is obscuration created through their own karma. He prayed that on attaining realization, he would be able to purify all beings by emanating a form abiding in front of or above each being and purifying obscurations with his light rays and amrita. When the Bodhisattva Tara was born as the daughter of a merchant, she realized that although many Bodhisattvas appear in male bodies, there are virtually none emanating as females. So she made a strong prayer of aspiration that until samsara was empty, she would work ceaselessly in female form to liberate sentient beings, and because of her strong aspiration, Tara is still considered a very great deity today.

Tara still manifests even in our own times, and it is impossible to say which women are her manifestations. Some may be prostitutes, some may be ordinary people, some may be insane—we can never be sure if someone is an incarnation of Tara. When I went to New York City, people told me, "There are a lot of crazy women in this town." I had strong faith in some of these women and was sure that some of them were manifestations of Tara. One old woman I met on the streets of New York was going around with a large pushcart, collecting totally worthless things out of the garbage, and she had managed to fill her cart up with them. She had a very strange demeanor and seemed rather deranged. When I met her, she was trying to get the cart up off the road, but it was too heavy for her to manage by herself. She was asking passersby to help lift the cart, but nobody would listen to her because she looked crazy. So she signaled to me to come over and help her. I went over and we both got hold of the cart, lifted it up, and managed to get it off the road. Then she wanted to give me something for helping her—a pair of old shoes. I told her it was all right, I did not need the shoes, but she insisted. Then she said she wanted me to help her unload the cart, so we started taking all kinds of things out of it and arranging them neatly in front of the cart. The whole point of this was to get down somewhere into the bottom of the cart where the shoes were, but once we had gotten everything out, she said that I should take it all. Then I began to think that there must be something really special about her since she wanted to give me all this stuff. I said I did not want any of it and I could never have shifted it even if I had wanted it. But she insisted. She finally said, "If you will not take anything, then at least try the shoes on." So I took my shoes off and tried the other ones on. She tied them up for me—they looked quite nice, and she was satisfied. I took them off and gave them back to her, put my own shoes on, and walked away. There was really something special about that woman.

My general impulse is to like strange people. People may be good or clever or wise, but they all tend to be much the same. But when people are crazy or a little weird, it makes them somehow special, and I like that. Whether they are old or young, ugly or beautiful, does not matter much.

I saw another woman in New York who must have been some kind of emanation. She does not know me, but I certainly know her. She goes down the street carrying bags around her neck, maybe twenty or thirty of them. She wears so many bags, you can only see her head. A very good person.

Then there is a fellow called Mark in Honolulu. Mark seems to be some sort of Hindu, but it is hard to say what he really is. Mark is a farmer. Nobody gets along with him, and he does not get along with anyone. He is always angry with somebody. And his activities do not conform to the general norm. He never wears any clothes, for one thing. He comes into the temple there completely naked and does prostrations in front of the image. The women can shout and scream as much as they like and tell him to get out of the temple, but he pays no attention. He sits down and meditates right in the middle of the temple, and whether he is causing a disturbance does not bother him at all. I liked him very much, and we used to go everywhere together in Honolulu. He is totally unartificial, and totally himself.

People invited me to lunch a lot in Honolulu, and I always went with Mark. Mark knew I was under medical care and that I had to have special food. People would try to prepare food specially, and Mark would always get angry with them. He would tell them their food was no good and just full of chemicals—Mark was a natural-food fanatic, and he would never let me eat it. Mark would often prepare food for me himself, but I could never eat it. Mark never used salt; in fact, there were hundreds of things Mark never used. He would make a vast quantity of something vaguely like Tibetan tsampa for me to eat dry, and force me to eat all of it. He would never let me leave until I finished it. Mark was completely straightforward. He was almost like a siddha, he was so unartificial. At about five in the morning, he would pound on my door, and as soon as I would open it, he would shove a huge bowl of this stuff in my hands and leave immediately. When I saw Mark for the last time, I told him I would always remember the three natural things he had taught me—natural food, natural activity, and natural mind—and said I hoped we would meet again. If Mark were to begin practicing the Dharma, maybe he would get too many ideas and his mind would become artificial.

It sounds like he has a lot of ideas anyway, I mean about natural foods and everything. A siddha would be the same whether he ate chemicals or not.

There are many different levels of insight. Just because insight is gained on one level does not mean freedom is attained in every sense.

If Dharma is to spread in the West, people's abilities and qualities must be increased. If this happens, how will you benefit the East, where mental qualities have deteriorated and where there is as much poverty as there has always been?

To be able to benefit them, you must become a Buddha. There are three kinds of motivation: the shepherd, the boatman, and the king. Perhaps the king motivation is more applicable if you want to help people in the East.

But you have taken the Bodhisattva precepts, so even if you cannot really help beings until you have attained realization, you have got to help them anyway while you are on the path. So what are you going to do about it?

If you cannot help yourself, how can you help anyone else? It is best to work with your own mind, so if you can realize the nature of your own mind, then you can help all sentient beings. You will know where their minds are and you will know what they need to hear. But if you don't have any realization, how can you help anyone at all?

This is the king motivation, which is a viable approach. Nonetheless, the Bodhisattva vow means working to benefit sentient beings in any way possible.

But you are always saying not to make conceptual ideas, Rinpoche. If you are always creating conceptual ideas, how can you benefit beings?

There is no end to Dharma, and there is no end to ideas. Dharma does not just end with nonconceptuality. At the time of meditation, one should be nonconceptual, but when dealing with conceptuality one has to operate in terms of concepts. To expand this point, there seem to be many contradictions between the Hinayana and the Mahayana, and also between the Mahayana and the Vajrayana. It is possible to divide them up and make them totally separate, but they can also be put together and viewed as completely harmonious.

Yes, but that is all conceptual ideas. What good does it do to sit here and think about all this? We should just act in the situation when it occurs instead of thinking about it so much. You said we should not conceptualize in meditation, but then you said conceptual ideas are needed in some cases. What good is it to think about how to benefit beings in the West or in the East? It does not do any good at all—you should just help beings whenever you can.

In order to get to the point of nonconceptuality, you first have to create concepts. We all met here today because the word was spread around yesterday. If this had not happened, we would never have come here today, unless we had made the decision in a previous life. I do not know how to benefit people in a worldly sense, but to benefit people in a Dharma sense, close association between people and contact between minds are necessary. If people who are involved in Dharma can make this close contact, possibly we can spread this principle of nonconceptuality. And if we could really do this, the world would be able to do without wars since people would stop making so many discriminations about things. As long as we benefit people in a worldly sense, they continue to have lots of different notions, they make laws, and they create fixed situations. Even if they say they are not being discriminative, people maintain their conceit about their own greatness. The West thinks it is great because of its development, and that people in other parts of the world are like savages, and the East thinks Westerners are untrustworthy thieves. This mistrust causes a lot of trouble. If we can benefit each other in a spiritual sense through personal contact, then possibly we can do something for the world. I am only one person and I do not feel able to do much in this sense, but you are many and I hope you will be able to do something positive.

11 · Ethics without Concepts

It is a tradition in Tibetan Buddhism to circumambulate holy objects such as stupas as a mark of respect, and Tibetans consider this a form of virtuous action. Here in Boudhanath many people follow this custom. We can see people walking around the Great Stupa at all times of day. But we do not often see great Lamas or Westerners circumambulating. Why is that?

For one thing, it is not a Western custom. Westerners do not think it is particularly virtuous or religious to walk round a stupa. And when great Lamas circumambulate, people come in hordes to receive blessings, so it gets very difficult for the Lamas.

Lamas would not be mobbed if they circumambulated the stupa as often as ordinary people. People would be used to seeing them. Great Lamas only attract a lot of attention because their presence around the stupa is rather rare.

Many of my teachers have emphasized taking teachings or doing formal meditation rather than circumambulating. I have the preconception that I should be getting somewhere when I am walking, but I never seem to get anywhere when I circumambulate—just back to where I started. But when I am meditating, I do not have that feeling; there seems to be something real there.

There are two modes of virtuous action: conceptual and nonconceptual. Nonconceptual virtuous action involves the direct use of fundamental awareness, and so is impossible for us at this stage; without having developed the experience of fundamental awareness, it is not possible to approach the nonconceptual mode of virtuous action.

Although the other mode of virtuous action is based on conceptuality and does not include wisdom, nonetheless it leads toward an understanding of fundamental awareness. This is like trying to communicate the realized nature. The realized nature itself cannot be directly expressed since it is beyond all conceptions, but the question does not have to stop there. Although the realized nature itself cannot be expressed, some idea of it can be communicated through metaphor. In the same way, although the conceptual mode of virtuous action does not use the wisdom nature, it orients us in that direction and enables us to approach realization.

Buddha Shakyamuni spoke very highly of nonconceptual virtuous action. He often said that meditating on emptiness for the duration of a finger-snap is better than performing conceptual virtuous action for many lifetimes. But he did not always teach in that way. At other times he said that attempting abstract meditation without awareness would just lead to a dull, unaware state of mind and would eventually result in rebirth as an animal. Therefore, he emphasized that wrong meditation is of no benefit at all, and for this reason he taught the conceptual modes of virtuous action, which bring us close to the fundamental understanding.

Conceptual modes of virtuous action may seem to be no more than mental activities, but they have considerable importance. There is a structure in these mental activities; they can be bad or good, and they can give a positive or a negative orientation. Until meditation is strongly developed, it is necessary to continue to use conceptual virtuous action when not engaged in abstract meditation. If we do not practice either level of virtuous action, we are in no sense practicing the Dharma, whatever we may think. Atisha said that until we reach the end of all concepts, we will continue to be involved in the structure of karma and to experience karmic results. As long as we are still involved in concepts and experiencing karmic results, we must use concepts in order to progress on the path.

Both modes of virtuous action, the conceptual in activity and the non-conceptual in meditation, are important on the path. It is not possible to give up conceptual virtuous action just by hearing the word "meditation," and it is not possible to rely completely on ordinary concepts and give up meditation, the source of final realization. Ordinary concepts involve ideas of bad and good, notions of creating suffering and happiness, but when an understanding of the realized condition is reached, the structure of hope and fear present in ordinary mind vanishes and there are no longer any hopes for better conditions or fears of worse ones. All conditions appear the same.

If we rely exclusively on the conceptual mode of virtuous action, we may certainly accumulate a lot of merit and orient ourselves favorably with regard to realization, but it is also possible that a lot of the accumulated merit will be wasted. If we fail to develop meditation, we might come to regret having performed so much virtuous action, and so destroy the merit. Without the practice of meditation, we will not be able to understand the evenness of all conditions. We will tend to discriminate between conditions, disliking the bad and preferring the good, and in this way fall into the trap of grasping at duality. Only through the practice of meditation can we avoid discrimination and understand the fundamental nature.

Trust in the mind. Avoid the eternalist view that there are creator gods who manipulate their creations, and the nihilist view that nothing really exists at all. While it is true that there is no ultimate reality in anything, it is important to trust in the fundamental basis of all experience, the in-itself quality of the mind. Only through the recognition of this self-nature can we attain freedom.

There is in our psyche a dualizing structure that isolates the experiencing individual from the objectified realm, the environment of experience. Whether or not we believe it, there is a causal event structure that contains the potential for unvirtuous action leading to unhappy results and virtuous action leading to good results. If we transcend grasping at the duality of subject and object, we will reach the state beyond all conceptions, the state of a Buddha. Merely to have heard of this state beyond conceptions does us no good at all; we have to practice in order to realize it. Not only must we gain some basic intellectual understanding of this view, we must also meditate on it in order to develop the confidence of inherent insight. Without developing such confidence, we are completely lost and wander from one condition to another with no sense of orientation. If we do not develop this confidence, it makes no difference how much we hear about this view or how many teachings we take about it; it makes no difference how much our teachers talk about it or how much we read about it.

Without understanding the fundamental nature, we cannot know what will happen to us when we die or what kind of rebirth we will have. Even in this lifetime, conditions are unstable. Sometimes we find ourselves in good circumstances, we are happy, and everything seems to be going well. At such times it can be very difficult to maintain any meditation or any reference to the fundamental nature. This is due to our attachment to happiness and our tendency to allow it to excite us, and in this way we can very easily lose whatever reference we have to the fundamental nature. Similarly, we become attached to bad conditions by being concerned about them, and this is another way in which we can lose our reference to the fundamental nature.

A life spent in the practice of abstract meditation and in praying to be reborn in a Buddhafield gives some potential for a favorable rebirth. Recognizing the fundamental nature through meditation and developing some confidence in it leads to the understanding that there is no such thing as death and that the fundamental reference is beyond life and death. This gives a confidence that transcends death.

If some abstract, nonconceptual meditation can be maintained, no matter what positive conditions we meet, no matter how rich we become or how happy we are with friends, we will never grasp at these things as real or be deluded by them. If we arouse some confidence in the fundamental nature, then no matter what negative conditions we meet—suffering, disease, death, breaking off with friends—there will be no pain.

When experiencing good conditions, it is crucial to apply the appropriate antidote; maintaining our meditation throughout all conditions constitutes the antidote to whatever conditions we may meet. If we do not apply the Dharma antidote to good conditions when they occur, they will become a source of suffering through their impermanence. An antidote must also be applied to negative conditions. Applying an antidote to conditions of suffering enables us to use negative conditions as the path by transforming them into positive conditions through reference to the fundamental nature.

At whatever level we approach the teaching, it is necessary to apply the appropriate antidote to our experience. Even with no development in meditation, we can apply a simple antidote. We can remember, for example, that pride is a negative thing and that it is not good to allow ourselves to be controlled by it. Pride is a defilement and leads to the creation of bad karma and to suffering both for ourselves and for other sentient beings, so it should be given up. If we know how to use defilement itself as an antidote, however, we can leave the defiled mind as it is, without having to do anything to it and without any idea of altering it. In this way defilement can be used as a means.

There are many different kinds of antidotes. There is the antidote of repenting or regretting a defilement, and there are the antidotes taught both in Buddhism and in various schools of Western psychology, according to which whatever energies one feels should not be repressed but should be expressed immediately. If one feels anger, for instance, one should give it expression, and if one feels desire, one should express that also. The immediate and unrepressed expression of these energies will rid one of the feelings. But these types of antidote have their limitations. Expressing defiled energy may make one feel better, and it may rid one of a particular feeling, but it does not necessarily help in social terms. Expressing anger may make someone else angry, and that person may cause trouble. Repenting for a defilement is a viable antidote also, but it is somewhat weak. To regret having given rise to a particular defilement may work for that particular instance, but the impulses will still continue to arise. One will have to keep applying the same antidote over and over again, and this will become a very busy process. Understanding how to use defilement as the path and how to relax the mind in the arising of defilement is the ultimate antidote, applicable to anything, and can lead to final realization.

If you find yourself getting angry with someone, do not allow the anger to control you and do not express it. Leave the mind in a relaxed and natural state, and you will not be controlled by any grasping at the duality of subject and object. Since you will not be concerned with any subject-object duality, your perception of an individual as a separate entity will vanish along with the aggression you felt. This will benefit you, of course, but the other person may feel that you have not responded adequately, and if he was angry to begin with, this may make him even angrier. That is of little importance; in order for a karmic connection to be established between two people by anger, they must both get angry. Since the individual who maintains a meditative attitude creates no bad karma through anger, little karmic connection is created. The meditative attitude also expresses virtuous action through the practice of patience.

No matter what experiences one meets, it is vital to apply an antidote immediately. It makes no difference which antidote one uses; the important thing is to utilize whatever conditions one encounters. The supreme antidote is meditating on the fundamental nature through all conditions, but without clear recognition of the fundamental nature, there is the danger of falling into dullness, the recognition of nothing whatsoever. In this dull state one would resemble a cow, which has little recognition of anything external to itself. Because of this danger it is important to follow a Lama and work toward the fundamental understanding.

Even without an accurate perception of the fundamental nature, it is still possible to work with antidotes. If I were very close to someone, I might become attached to him and to his kindness to me. How could I deal with that situation if I had no meditation? I could apply a conceptual antidote to my feelings of attachment. I could think, "This person has been good to me for a long time and I have become attached to him, but perhaps he is going to be bad to me. Maybe he is just trying to get something out of me or cheat me somehow." I could think of a few negative things like that to counteract my attachment. And perhaps eventually my friend would actually start treating me badly, getting angry with me and giving me a hard time. At that point I might start hating him. Then I could apply an antidote to these feelings by telling myself that they were utterly irrational, based only on some momentary consideration, some ephemeral event, and since my friend had been good to me in the past, he could not really feel completely negative toward me now. I could go on applying such an antidote to my negative feelings again and again. This sort of antidote can be used even if one does not understand the fundamental nature.

Antidotes should be used whatever our circumstances, but we should not talk about them to others. They should remain entirely within our own consciousness. When enjoying good conditions with friends or lovers, for example, in the company of great Lamas, or when enjoying good food, an antidote should be applied to feelings of attachment; so both good and bad conditions can be used in the practice of the Dharma. What we have to look for in all these conditions is the state of evenness.

Buddhahood means not abiding in any extreme and not making any judgments about anything whatever. This means not holding to any opinion at all, and if we can abide in this state without any fixed decisions about the nature of phenomena, the mind will remain in a condition of evenness. We will be able to work constructively with any kind of impulse in any kind of situation, and since this evenness leads to a bliss beyond ordinary unhappiness and happiness, we will be happy even if our conditions are entirely negative. Once this evenness has been developed we will no longer be controlled by conditions. Even if the mind gives rise to negative impulses, we will be able to transform them into pure impulses. We will have total freedom in working with conditions.

This does not mean that we should not be attached to conditions at all. When we start to practice, it is necessary to seek a suitable environment and to associate with people who have pure minds and some inclination toward the Dharma. Through contact with such people, we will tend to develop some orientation toward Dharma ourselves. If we habitually associate with people who lack a pure-minded orientation, we may be drawn away from Dharma. In the beginning we are controlled by circumstances to quite a high degree, so it is difficult to give up discrimination about them. This does not mean, of course, that we should cultivate a bias toward Tibetans or Westerners, toward people involved in Dharma or those not involved. We must learn how to practice without preference for any condition, and how to utilize whatever conditions we meet so that they become irrelevant to practice. We must remember also that good conditions can be very dangerous—they are the source of bad conditions. Any good conditions we meet are subject to change, and it is easy to become so accustomed to them that we are incapable of functioning in bad conditions. Therefore, it is important to develop the ability to work with all conditions. This ability comes with the reference to the fundamental in-itself quality, and from this reference we can work with conditions without being controlled or influenced by them.

12 · Games

In ancient times Dharma was widely spread in the East and many people had great faith in it. Nowadays, however, times are bad. Many people are unable to apply the teachings of Dharma to their own minds and so have little faith in it anymore; some even abandon it completely. The younger generation of Tibetans in particular has less faith in Dharma than their parents. However, Westerners can be of great service to Dharma, and I hope that some of you will be able to act. People have different motivations, of course, so perhaps it will not be possible for all of you to benefit Dharma and help sentient beings in that way.

It is a mistake to think that Dharma can only be learned from Easterners. Many Easterners today feel that they should be more self-reliant, particularly in the political sphere. They are concerned to grow their own food, build their own airplanes, and be independent of the West. They usually find this rather difficult, however, which embarrasses them to some extent. This sort of attitude is irrelevant to the Dharma; one should never discriminate between peoples and countries. We should not feel that a particular country is full of savages and that there is no hope of learning anything from there, and we should not be concerned about the ethnic origin of a Dharma teacher. Any place in which Dharma is taught is an appropriate field of study, and any teacher with the necessary qualities is appropriate, regardless of his ancestry. We should learn Dharma wherever we can, seeking it wherever we can find it, without regard to social circumstances. At this time, Dharma teaching seems to be concentrated in the East, which means that the East is an appropriate place to seek teachings. But if Dharma becomes established in the West, then Europe or America may become the center of Dharma teaching, and Easterners may go there in search of the true teachings. One should never apply political attitudes to Dharma; Dharma is quite different from politics.

Considerable interest in the Tibetan traditions of Buddhism has evolved recently in the West. Before that, apart from a few students of Zen, Westerners had virtually no interest at all in Buddhism, largely because of the predominating influence of nihilistic philosophical systems. But eventually one or two scholars were drawn to take an interest in Buddhism. This interest gradually widened, and now many people have a high regard for Buddhism, particularly in its Tibetan forms. Dharma is beginning to spread in the West, and things have reached the point where it is getting involved with politics; in some areas the two are even becoming confused. This political influence on Dharma is chiefly the result of conditions in the places where Dharma is being spread and has nothing to do with Dharma itself. Unfortunately there is no way this can be avoided. The world is pervaded by legal systems, and we are obliged to follow them; otherwise we are liable to be imprisoned. We are involved in society and so must obey its laws. A number of Lamas have been criticized recently for their involvement in political affairs, but this criticism is rather meaningless. We are living in an age in which politics is important, and some people have no choice but to become involved in politics. Such criticism of Lamas should be ignored. It would be excellent if all the Dharma practitioners throughout the world could live in the mountains and caves like Milarepa and be free of all need, but this is not possible. They would get hungry without food, they would get cold without clothes, and in order to acquire these things they have to live in society, take an active part in it, and obey its laws. It is best to be free of political involvement when practicing Dharma, but there is no reason to make judgments about anyone else's involvement in politics.

Even though it has nothing to do with Dharma, I have mentioned politics here because we are all involved in society and consequently have many hopes and fears about the state of the world. These hopes and fears can be an obstacle to practice.

It is vital to practice in a stable manner. There is a great tendency nowadays in both East and West to nibble at Dharma, to find out what it is all about and then forget about it. Sometimes people even abandon Dharma altogether as a result of this dilettante attitude and later defame those from whom they had received teachings. We should never allow ourselves to drift into this sort of attitude, but should constantly persevere with Dharma. If we approach Dharma with the idea of just taking a nibble, it is better never to start taking teachings at all.

There is no need to spend a lot of money on Dharma. The important thing is to continue with the practice and develop the qualities of Dharma, and this will be of benefit to other sentient beings as well as to ourselves. It is fine to put money into Dharma in one way or another, but there is no real need to do so.

Always maintain a stable attitude toward the teacher. Many people have doubts about their teacher, and they increase these doubts by talking about them to other people. By feeding their doubts in this way, they tend to break their connection with the teacher, and once that connection is broken, the fundamental wisdom cannot be communicated, and so wisdom mind cannot be developed.

Dharma is the only thing that will be of any use to us when we die. Nihilistic philosophies offer no real solution to the problem of death, and do not have any real relation to it. Even in this lifetime Dharma is of ultimate benefit. When we find ourselves in conditions of suffering, parents and friends are of little help and can even become sources of further suffering. The real meaning of Dharma is the transformation of suffering into happiness, using both negative and positive conditions for the attainment of freedom. Therefore, whatever we experience in the world should be used in the practice of Dharma. If we develop good qualities, we should not become proud of them, and we should avoid falling into ignorance when meditating. If you attain some development of bodhichitta through your practice, you will be able to benefit people in your own countries when you leave here, and so free them from suffering.

It is often said that certain places are particularly beneficial for meditation practice—Sarnath, Bodhgaya, and Benares, for example, and Boudhanath as well. And you said that there is merit to be gained by walking around the Great Stupa. When I was back in the States, I used to do my shopping in supermarkets, and it happened that the shelves were arranged in such a way that I would have to walk around them clockwise, as one would circumambulate a stupa. I cannot imagine that there is any special power emanating from the produce on supermarket shelves, but I have been told that it is important to circumambulate stupas clockwise. Can you clarify this for me?

It does not matter where we meditate once our practice is established. If our meditation is stable we can take it with us wherever we go; the Three Jewels and the blessings of the meditation go with us everywhere. In that sense it does not matter where we are, but this does not deny the benefit of auspicious places. Such places have been consecrated by the great Buddhas and siddhas of the past and offer very favorable circumstances for meditation practice. We can develop as much meditation in one day in those places as we could in a month elsewhere, because they have become focal points for the blessings of the teachers. But if we are not able to stay in such places—due to lack of funds, for example—there is nothing to worry about. The blessings of whatever practice we have developed will accompany us wherever we go.

Eastern people tend to have a very deep-rooted character. Their basic intentions are not easily changed, their decisions are very fixed, and they consider their actions very deeply. These tendencies can be an obstacle or they can be beneficial: a bad person will consistently be bad and a good person consistently good. By contrast, Westerners tend to be speedy. They boil over like a pot of boiling water, and everything flows out before they have had time to examine it. They seldom seem to reach stable decisions or form stable relationships. There is a way of life between these two extremes, although I have not found it—I have the Western type of boiling nature.

Pride is a great obstacle, but we should not attempt to repress it. We should use it. This does not imply giving expression to it but means using it in such a way that the tendency toward pride gradually diminishes. A proud person uses his pride to shut off the world. This makes him incapable of recognizing positive qualities in other people and so unable to develop such qualities himself. He is like a person with high blood pressure, eyes full of blood and unable to see properly. A proud person also expresses his pride, and this makes people avoid him. His connection with other sentient beings is severed, and they are unable to help him in any way. We should use pride by applying the appropriate antidote instead of expressing it and being controlled by it. In this way we will preserve our connection with sentient beings and will be able to develop in Dharma.

I spoke the other day about the different antidotes one can apply to the defilements. If a doctor or an engineer became proud of his skills, he might apply the antidote of remembering that there are others more learned and skillful than he is. If he allowed himself to become proud, he would repel people and they would take their business elsewhere. This is an ordinary sort of antidote; a meditator would apply a different antidote to pride. He would not repress it when it arose or allow it any expression, but would just watch it. Since pride has no solidity, watching causes it to vanish, and the meditator does not have to do anything about it.

In happy conditions we should remember that happiness is impermanent, and suffering is inevitable in samsara; so in good circumstances we should practice meditation. Initially we are compelled to use the conceptual mode of virtuous action, but we should try to transform the conceptual mode into the nonconceptual. In the same way, we should try to transform suffering into happiness, and happiness into nonconceptual happiness.

Is there such a thing in Buddhist terms as lack of pride constituting a defilement—insecurity and self-hatred?

The antidote to self-hatred is looking for the self you hate. As soon as you feel self-hatred arising, look at yourself. Above all, relax. If you do not relax, there can be no Dharma. Everything is just child's play; there is no need to take anything seriously. Some people are bad and some are good, some people fight and steal and hate—it is all just games. Do not take any of it seriously.

Is the Dharma just game-playing?

Grasping at Dharma inevitably blocks the path to attaining realization. Saraha said that whatever one is attached to is a demon. But in a sense we must be attached to Dharma because it is impossible to practice without faith. Ultimately, however, there can be no attachment to the Dharma, for attachment will prevent the realization of fundamental awareness. No teaching will lead to realization if approached with a grasping or attached attitude, but at our stage of development it may perhaps be best to treat Dharma as an object.

We should leave phenomena just as they are, without meddling with them in any way. However, since we are caught in the trap of dualistic mind, we must work within that frame of reference by practicing conceptual virtuous action. We might think that there is no reality anywhere, that nothing really exists; but if someone stuck a needle in our thigh, it would hurt. Experiencing this pain proves that we are still involved in grasping at duality and have not understood the fundamental nature, whatever fantasies we may have to the contrary.

Never abandon the practice of Dharma. Continue to practice, but do not allow yourself to become attached to any practice. By watching the world as if it were just a child's game, it is easy to progress in Dharma.

Should we try to gain some intellectual understanding of reincarnation, or just get on with the practice and wait till an intuitive understanding grows?

As long as we continue to have dualistic conceptions, we continue to create habits. This can be understood in terms of dreams. We create habits constantly as we live through our day, and at night we fall asleep and experience dreams involving these same habits. There is nothing real in these dreams, but they appear real because of our dualizing conceptions. We have been caught in this structure since the beginninglessness of all our lifetimes and have built up countless habits through our dualizing. Habits continue to arise as the appearance of sentient beings and their realms of existence; that is what reincarnation is about. There is no real realm, but due to our habits there seems to be something real.

The final antidote to grasping at duality is attainment of Buddhahood. In order to realize Buddhahood we must start by praying to some expression of enlightenment, such as a Buddha or a deity. This is the frame of reference we have to work with, caught as we are in a dualizing structure. Starting from this conceptual frame of reference, we practice meditation in order to develop that insight which is beyond grasping at duality. This can lead to the realization of the state beyond duality and free us from habits and incessant rebirth.

When we were meditating earlier, there were trucks passing in the street outside, car horns blowing, and children shouting. Did you hear them?

Of course.

Then you were not meditating very well.

Yogis in Tibet did not hear car horns, so I suppose they must have meditated very well.

People in Tibet had no habits about cars, so they never conceived of them. When I was young I had no habits about cars, and in fact I never saw any. Now that I have come here, my habits have changed and I see cars all the time. Everything around us is created by the force of our own habits. Even Bodhisattvas have habits until they transcend the tenth level; only Buddhas are completely free of habits.

We should avoid treating phenomenal appearances as real in any way. When we see a teapot, for example, we should look at the mind rather than the teapot. When we see a beautiful woman, we identify her and we think, "That's Gretyl." This is a mistake. Seeing Gretyl and thinking of her as Gretyl gives us a lot of desire, and we feel the impulse to grab hold of her. This is entirely the wrong approach. We should look instead at the mind that perceives Gretyl, try to discover where that mind is, and so see the emptiness of that particular perception. This will lead to the perception of the inseparability of appearance and emptiness, the nature of realization. This does not mean that we should avoid any kind of activity whatever. As long as the mind remains in meditation, lifestyle is unimportant.

All phenomena are an aspect of the mandalas of the deities, and yet all perceptions are in the mind. Does it follow that the mandalas of the deities are entirely within the mind?

The highest tantras teach that the mandalas of the deities are all part of the mind. They teach that when one expands and expresses the mandala, it is in the mind, and when one reabsorbs it, the reabsorbed mandala is in the mind. Thus it is of great benefit to watch the mind when pride, anger, or jealousy arises. When we become excited or experience many desires, it is beneficial to recall the stories of Lamas and yogis who went through great hardship. This will enable us to maintain an even state of mind; it will make the mind humble and peaceful. When feeling sad or depressed, we should expand the mind, trying to step out of our own circumstances.

Other people manage to enjoy themselves; they get drunk and have a good time, so why can't we? There is never any reason to keep the mind tight and depressed. This is a very common approach to solving the problem of depression, although meditation is a much more profound and effective antidote.

Few people in the West have any knowledge of the Tibetan language, so it is often necessary for interpreters to fly over from the East. Suppose a Westerner who had lived in the East long enough to acquire a good knowledge of Tibetan were asked to visit the West as an interpreter. If he has developed some meditation, he would have no fears about this prospect and would not be subject to pride. But if he had not developed much meditation, he might become anxious. He might think, "I have been out in the East all this time, while these people here in the West have been attending universities and institutes—they probably know a lot more than I do." And if the Westerners had not developed their meditation either, they might become anxious as well. They might think, "This man has been in the East for many years, and perhaps he knows more about Dharma than we do; perhaps his Tibetan is better than ours." This would produce tension and conflict. If the Westerners had not developed their meditation, they might try to flatter the interpreter, they might criticize him, or they might even get angry with him; and if the interpreter had no meditation, he might respond to this with pride or with anger. Rival factions might spring up, one supporting the interpreter, the other supporting the Westerners. The two groups would indulge in gossip and backbiting, and this might even result in violence. I very much hope that this sort of thing will never occur.

We should regard the world as no more than a game and should endeavor through meditation to develop profound qualities. Then neither criticism of our ignorance nor praise of our meditation will affect us, and our response will show whether our meditation is really developed.

An old man watching children playing has no hopes or fears about the outcome of their game. He is not personally involved, though he may be vaguely amused by the spectacle. This is the attitude we should take to the world, and this is why some Lamas and great siddhas spend a lot of time playing with children. Ordinary people think this sort of behavior is completely insane; such Lamas may be quite old, yet they go around playing with children as if they were children themselves. This can also happen as a result of senility, of course, but that is a different matter.

Back in the States I used to work on developing new techniques of language learning. One of the methods we came up with was using hypnosis to regress people to a point in childhood before they had built up many preconceptions, and in this way they were able to learn languages incredibly fast. They had virtually no preconceptions whatever. How should one go about playing with children? Should we involve established preconceptions?

When a child is playing, he is attached to the game; he has dual conceptions about the nature of the game and grasps at it. When a yogi plays with children, he has no grasping whatever toward their game, no attachment at all. If we saw a couple of children play-fighting in the street, we might think they were fighting in earnest and try to do something about it; but if we were free of attachment, we would have no conceptions about it at all, and we would not make any judgments one way or the other. Though if we do see children fighting, maybe it is best to stop them—we are still involved in dualistic mind and do not have this insight, and the children might well injure each other.

Is bodhichitta a dualistic conception?

There are two modes of bodhichitta. Ordinary bodhichitta is based on an experiential field toward which one feels love and compassion, and this dualistic mode of bodhichitta derives from ultimate bodhichitta beyond any such conception. It is the ultimate form of bodhichitta that must be understood. Ultimate bodhichitta is found only in Buddhahood, and until one reaches that level, it is necessary to utilize bodhichitta in its conceptual mode.

All the teachings of Dharma have these two modes: they can all be considered in their relative aspect or their ultimate aspect. On a relative level, America might be considered to be constituted of houses, cars, people, and so on; but if one were to look for the ultimate America in an individual, that American-ness could not be found. The compassion of the Buddha has no object and so is ultimate, but for the moment we must continue to operate in terms of relative bodhichitta, for there is no other way to approach the ultimate level of bodhichitta.

It seems that nobody here is particularly sectarian or overly proud, and that you have all taken a relaxed attitude to these discussions of ours. This is particularly fortunate. I have talked a little in structural terms in accordance with the scriptures and the ancient systems, and I have also talked about meditation in nonstructural terms. I have tried to use simple, ordinary language that people can relate to, and I feel that although we have only been here for a short period and only met a few times, perhaps we have been able to talk about a good many things. Everything I have been saying here is in harmony with Dharma. I have avoided a definition of what I have said so that it cannot be labeled as this teaching or that teaching from this sect or that sect.

Most of the Dharma people I met in the United States were disciples of my father, and because of this contact, quite often they would ask me to go along and talk, much as we have been doing. But here in Boudhanath, we all came together without very much formal organization and without any connection with any particular sect—it just happened. It seems to me that this must be due to good karma we created in the past.

BOOKS BY THINLEY NORBU

Echoes: The Boudhanath Teachings (2016)

Gypsy Gossip and Other Advice (2016)

A Brief Fantasy History of a Himalayan: Autobiographical Reflections (2015)

Sunlight Speech That Dispels the Darkness of Doubt: Sublime Prayers, Praises, and Practices of the Nyingma Masters (2015)

The Sole Panacea: A Brief Commentary on the Seven-Line Prayer to Guru Rinpoche That Cures the Suffering of the Sickness of Karma and Defilement (2014)

A Cascading Waterfall of Nectar (2006)

Welcoming Flowers from Across the Cleansed Threshold of Hope: An Answer to Pope John Paul II's Criticism of Buddhism (1997, 2014)

White Sail: Crossing the Waves of Ocean Mind to the Serene Continent of the Triple Gems (1992)

Magic Dance: The Display of the Self-Nature of the Five Wisdom Dakinis (1981, 1999)

The Small Golden Key to the Treasure of the Various Essential Necessities and Extraordinary Buddhist Dharma (1985, 1993)

Printed in the United States
By Bookmasters